MARBLEHEAD
LIGHTHOUSE
ON LAKE ERIE

OHIO'S HISTORIC BEACON

....

JAMES PROFFITT

THE
History
PRESS

Published by The History Press
Charleston, SC 29403
www.historypress.net

First published 2015

Manufactured in the United States

ISBN 978.1.46711.818.7

Library of Congress Control Number: 2015939218

CONTENTS

FOREWORD

The Marblehead Lighthouse, arguably the Midwest's single most recognizable structure, has been written about dozens, perhaps hundreds, of times throughout its 185-year history. These writings have appeared in local newspapers, statewide and Midwest tourist magazines, biweekly summer publications and journals of every description. Some of these stories are factual, some nearly so and many way off the mark. The lighthouse has been photographed and painted many times over. To date, the most comprehensive writing on the light is Betty Neidecker's *The Marblehead Lighthouse: Lake Erie's Eternal Flame*, published in 1995.

Until now, however, there has never been an in-depth treatment of the structure in the context of its place in the history of American lighthouses. James Proffitt, in his *Marblehead Lighthouse on Lake Erie: Ohio's Historic Beacon*, has done that. His study of the light is specific, detailed and interesting, but he goes beyond the local light, its keepers and builder to give us a comprehensive overview of the United States Lighthouse Service in its infancy up to current times. We are actually treated to a conversation between Hamilton and Washington concerning the need for a uniform policy governing the new nation's aids to commerce and transportation. Proffitt incorporates a detailed treatment of lighting technology, the coming of the Fresnel lens and tells us why the United State's reluctance to use the French innovation caused our lights to lag behind their European counterparts in intensity by decades. How did lighthouse policy affect the young nation's whaling industry? It's all in here. Are you curious about the origins of the United States Life-Saving

Service and its heroic underpinnings at the Marblehead Lighthouse? Then look no further. Are you interested in shipwrecks, salvage, tragic loss of life, heroic rescues and treks across the ice to assist a damsel in distress? You have come to the right source. From the day-to-day activities of the light's keepers down to the light's impact on present-day art and tourism, you will find it all here.

Last but certainly not least, Proffitt writes well, incorporating a free flow of ideas interspersed with but never overburdened by details and well-organized facts.

Enjoy your trip to the lighthouse; you will be rewarded.

PAUL C. MOON

Moon is president of the Ottawa County Historical Society; the great-great-great-great-grandson of Benajah Wolcott, the first keeper of the Marblehead Light; and the great-great-great grandson of William Kelly, its builder.

PREFACE

The Marblehead Lighthouse, constructed in 1821, is the oldest continuously operated lighthouse on the Great Lakes. While human and natural forces have transformed many American lighthouses, the beacon that has guided mariners on Lake Erie's Western Basin for almost two centuries remains largely unchanged.

That's not to say it hasn't been challenged by nature and people—it most certainly has. And through it all, the structure has remained intact since its birth from the hands of a local craftsman. While the light sources, keepers, custodians and mariners associated with the lighthouse have all changed many times over, the lighthouse and the scenic limestone outcrop it stands on remain firm—and much loved—and are as much an integral part of quality of life for local residents, Ohioans and tourists as they have been a navigational aid since the lighthouse's erection.

History surrounding the Marblehead Lighthouse has one particularly noteworthy distinction: the heroic actions of local residents Lucien, Ai and Hubbard Clemons were so noteworthy that the very first Gold Life-Saving Medals were awarded to the trio. A short time later, Lucien was placed in charge of the new United States Life-Saving Service station, erected nearby, at Point Marblehead.

Today, the lighthouse, the current keeper's house (which stands in its shadow) and the very first keeper's personal home (which is located a few miles away), are hubs of community activity and beacons of history, education

The official insignia of the United States Life-Saving Service. *Courtesy of the USCG.*

and tourism. At the time of publication, a local historical society is making plans for a groundbreaking ceremony that will precede the construction of a replica of the first lifesaving station, which was built almost 150 years ago.

ACKNOWLEDGEMENTS

The assistance of many individuals and organizations was crucial in writing this book. I would like to thank the Marblehead Lighthouse Historical Society, the Ottawa County Historical Museum, the National Archives, the Lakeside Heritage Society, Phil Teitlebaum, the Rutherford B. Hayes Presidential Center, Chaz Avery, the Ida Rupp Public Library, Boyd Weber and Rick Henkel, among others. And especially, Rebecca Lawrence-Weden, Dianne M. Rozak and Paul C. Moon.

INTRODUCTION

T his is *my* lighthouse!"
I have heard those words one hundred times. The beloved Marblehead Lighthouse is known as the most photographed site in the state of Ohio. No doubt it also is the most visited landmark, as this charismatic light station draws over one million people each year. It is romantic, captivating and iconic. Set on a limestone ridge just above the shore of the great Lake Erie, it is truly a light for all seasons and a magnet of charm for all reasons. The attraction is simple: it's a real lighthouse. You can touch it. You can climb it. You *will* fall in love with it.

Tears of joy and of sadness have dampened the grounds over the nearly two hundred years this historic beacon has been lit. Flowers have become symbolic here. The waves carry them away from the shore as saddened families remember those they lost. Flowers are tossed to waiting hands while a new bride smiles in front of the tower. They are silently placed on a memorial brick. They are mysteriously tucked between the rocks, along with a handwritten note. And dedicated volunteers lovingly plant them each season.

Much happens here. Friendships are made, vows are exchanged, memories begin, dreams are shared, traditions commence, steps are climbed and fears are overcome.

For many years, I have been given the opportunity to spend six days a week each summer greeting visitors to the lighthouse. It has been a pleasure to see not only our returning guests but also those experiencing the lighthouse for the first time. I often say each day here is new. The sky is never the same, the wind constantly changes and the lake offers countless unanticipated pleasures.

The Marblehead Lighthouse is much more than just a great photograph; it is a place where you can energize your soul. Once you visit, I'm confident it will become your lighthouse too!

DIANNE M. ROZAK
Ohio Department of Natural Resources naturalist, Marblehead Lighthouse State Park

Chapter 1

THE FOUNDATION

The Marblehead Lighthouse, originally known as the Sandusky Bay Light Station, is situated just a few yards from the water. During nor'easters, Lake Erie's muddied, surly waters lap at its base, and crashing waves surround the rocky point in walls of ice-cold spray. Despite a seemingly low-lying, vulnerable location, the designers and builders of the lighthouse were wise enough to choose a location well suited for such a structure, and they built the light tower of the highest quality materials and with the most talented labor.

The lighthouse was placed on a solid outcrop of the Columbus limestone formation, a massive section of limestone that runs from central Ohio, near the state capital, north, beneath Lake Erie. Like the Danbury Peninsula, the Lake Erie islands—including Kelleys Island, Johnson's Island, the Bass Islands and Pelee—are all high points of the formation, first named by a Columbus scientist.

The limestone in the formation dates to the Middle Devonian age, about 350 million years ago. At that time, what is now Ohio was located south of the equator, at about the same latitude as Tahiti, and surrounded by a warm, shallow ocean of clean, crystal-clear water.

The stone itself was formed from lime-rich mud on the sea floor that was subjected to lithification—that is, compressed by other rocky formations that layered themselves atop the lime-rich deposits beneath. Over hundreds of millions of years, the immense pressure turned the mud into solid, virtually indestructible limestone. While dinosaurs roamed the earth's landmasses during the Mezozoic period, Ohio was buried, and the limestone was being slowly formed.

About 65 million years ago, erosion exposed the long-buried stone. That's when massive glaciers moved into the area, gouging Lakes Superior, Ontario, Michigan, Huron and Erie out of the earth's surface and leaving expansive limestone formations behind. In *The History of the Firelands*, published in 1873, the peninsula is described this way:

> *The eastern portion of the township of Danbury is underlain by a strata of limestone rock, filled with fossils. Over several hundred acres in the center of the east part of the peninsula, the limestone rock is entirely uncovered, or at best covered with a scant soil, which produces very little vegetation. With this exception the soil is very productive. There are deep grooves cut in this limestone formation, in some places wide enough to allow of a wagon being driven.*

The natural foundation the lighthouse rests on is the best. Without pilings, boulders, riprap or other manmade reinforcements, the structure is firmly situated on tried-and-tested, eons-old limestone. The location of the lighthouse—the entrance of Sandusky Bay at the southeastern tip of the South Passage, the lake between the Ohio mainland and the Lake Erie islands—takes a heavy beating in late autumn, winter and early spring each year. More than 250 miles of open, unobstructed water lies to the northeast of the lighthouse. As waves reach the peninsula they rise as the lake, nearing the Western Basin, becomes considerably shallower than the Central and Eastern Basins.

Harry H. Ross wrote in his 1949 book *Enchanting Isles of Lake Erie*, "Sandusky Bay is so shallow in places in midsummer that when the water is exceptionally low and calm, one can walk on a sandbar from the Marblehead shoreline about to the Cedar Point channel (to the east), skirting the west shore of Cedar Point, in water a few inches deep."

During certain weather events, the Marblehead Peninsula receives the highest waves on Lake Erie. The long distance the lake stretches, all the way from Buffalo, means the lighthouse's natural limestone underpinnings have taken brutal punishments through nearly two centuries of service. Visitors to the lighthouse will find an interesting and, when wet, slippery foundation. The stone near the shore is often covered with mosses and lichens.

The limestone base has numerous joints, or fissures. The cracks are caused by water that seeps into stone and then freezes. While it has weakened

Deep cracks in the limestone near the lighthouse base continue to form but have not affected the almost two-century-old structure. *Author's photo.*

shorelines in other areas, the joints near the base of the Marblehead Lighthouse have not appeared to affect the stability of the structure, despite their number and depths.

In addition to the joints, visitors may find a number of fossils. The remnants of early sea life include the clam-like brachiopod; tiny groups of corals, called colonial corals; now-extinct snails, clams and mollusks; and an occasional trilobite.

In the past, scientists with the United States Geological Survey (USGS) have used the lighthouse as an observation point to study ice movement in the area. One former USGS employee, a now-retired Ohio State University professor, said he believes that the lake ice pushed toward shore during thaws has, in fact, actually touched the lighthouse in the past. While no photographic evidence proves this, anyone who has visited the site during late winter or early spring thaws can easily imagine the ice being pushed far onshore. At times, sheets and chunks of ice more than twenty feet in diameter and two or more feet thick have towered dozens of feet above the water level. At least one keeper made a diary entry describing ice approaching and surrounding the base of the tower.

Chapter 2
A YOUNG NATION'S LIGHTS

The first firmly evidenced navigational aid in colonial America was a small stone tower erected in 1673 at Nantasket, Massachusetts. The site, a promontory guarding the south approach to Boston Harbor, featured "fier-bales of pitch and ocum" in an iron basket. Citizens of the community provided funds to operate the beacon.

The first recorded lighthouse was constructed of rubble stone on Little Brewster Island in Boston Harbor. In 1716, the Province of Massachusetts Bay paid £2,285 to build the structure. The province paid Little Brewster's light keeper, George Worthington, £50 annually. Subsequently, other colonies established lighthouses to aid maritime navigation. During that time, customs collectors often imposed "light dues" based on the tonnage of vessels utilizing the ports where lights were located.

In the 1700s, after the British defeated the French and their Indian allies in the decades-long French and Indian War, the East Coast and the lands west were available for expansion as the population of the English colonies swelled. Toward the end of the eighteenth century, colonists broke away from their great European benefactor, which had become less and less friendly toward its overseas subjects. The Revolutionary War saw the United States of America emerge as a republic, independent of England's rule, and a burgeoning nation of trade.

More lighthouses had been erected on the Atlantic coast. America's leaders decided that operation of the sites was critical to the young nation's successful commerce, and so they moved to organize the operation of the lighthouses.

In August 1789, the fledgling United States Congress passed the Lighthouse Act. Officially, it was the Act for the Establishment and Support of Lighthouses, Beacons, Buoys and Public Piers. This legislation, the ninth official act ever passed by Congress, was the very first public works act. Thus, the United States Lighthouse Establishment was created; it fell under jurisdiction of the Department of the Treasury. The bill read, in part:

> *All expenses which shall accrue from and after the fifteenth day of August one thousand seven hundred and eighty-nine, in the necessary support, maintenance and repairs of all lighthouses, beacons, buoys and public piers erected, placed, or sunk before the passing of this act, at the entrance of, or within any bay, inlet, harbor, or port of the United States, for rendering the navigation thereof easy and safe, shall be defrayed out of the Treasury of the United States.*

The act stated that the twelve existing lighthouses, which had been established and operated individually by colonies and states, be transferred to the control of the federal government. The states, however, failed to abide by the decision until eight years later because they distrusted the power of a central government. By 1800, the nation boasted twenty-four lighthouses owned and operated by the federal government along the Atlantic coast. Control of the lighthouses was assigned to Alexander Hamilton, who was appointed the nation's first secretary of the treasury, a month after the Lighthouse Act was passed.

Hamilton told President George Washington that lighthouse service should be free and that lighthouse dues should be waived. Washington agreed, and the fees paid by vessel operators utilizing lights at United States ports were abolished. Hamilton strongly believed that navigation tools for commercial vessels in American ports could only benefit the nation. Hamilton felt the movement of goods into and out of America—including the nation's deep interior territories, which were about to be settled—should be a vital concern to its leaders and citizens. Lake Erie, along with the other Great Lakes, was a soon-to-be-exploited resource. After assuming responsibility for lighthouses, Hamilton spent a great deal of time compiling information, reports and recommendations.

Whatever the United States did in its earliest construction of lighthouses, it did right. Out of the first eleven federal lighthouses that Hamilton persuaded Congress to build, nine are still standing. During the first twenty-one years of overseeing lighthouses, the federal government passed

A view from the interior of the tower illustrates how thick the walls are. *Author's photo.*

control of the nation's navigational aids around enough times to make a historian's head spin. The Lighthouse Service's operations were transferred to the just-created Commissioner of Revenue in 1792. After that office was abolished just ten years later, lighthouses were transferred back to the treasury. But eleven years later, in 1813, the Commissioner of Revenue was reestablished, and lighthouse operations returned to that position's control. After the Commissioner of Revenue was again abolished four years later, oversight returned again to the treasury. In 1820, when the act to abolish the Commissioner of Revenue took effect, lighthouse oversight found a more permanent home under Stephen Pleasonton, the United States Treasury's fifth auditor.

During this time, maritime traffic on the Great Lakes had increased dramatically as the nation's population increased and pushed steadily westward. But the freshly minted nation, forged from British colonies just a few decades earlier, would soon enter another war with England. That conflict would put the brakes on westward expansion in the region.

The Marblehead Lighthouse's first keeper was Benajah Wolcott. According to historical accounts, he was the first white settler in what is now Ottawa County. Wolcott was a true American patriot, born a British subject and dying an American war veteran and employee of the federal government. Wolcott was born in New Haven, Connecticut, in 1762 to a long line of mariners. Wolcott's maternal family was descended from William Brewster, leader of the Mayflower Company. His family supported the colonists' break with England, and Benajah enlisted to fight as a teenager, serving until the war ended. Wolcott served in several posts, including direct service beneath both Anthony Wayne and George Washington.

Both of Wolcott's parents died during the 1780s, and court records indicate their financial situation was not great and that collections were made against the estate. Wolcott signed onto one of President Washington's state militias and was appointed a lieutenant in October 1793 in Albany County, New York. But in April 1796, he "refuse[d] to equip himself." It is speculated that this led to his leaving military service.

But before settling on the western frontier, the Connecticut native first saw the land as part of an initial survey crew in a special territory called the Firelands. The area was so-named because of events that had transpired decades earlier more than five hundred miles east. In 1777, British troops and loyalists attacked and destroyed businesses, public buildings, homes, churches and schools in Danbury, Connecticut. Later, they repeated the moves in Norwalk, Fairfield, New London, Greenwich and other communities in the state. Many citizens of the new nation suffered severe personal losses at the hands of the British and their supporters.

Later, the new state of Connecticut, in a bid to help those whose losses in the blazes were great, offered land grants to citizens who chose to leave the East Coast and take up residence in the state's vast tract of land known as the Western Reserve. In 1792, the Connecticut legislature offered a half million acres of the westernmost portion of its Western Reserve to such fire victims and settlers. Hence, the name Firelands and the large number of townships, villages and cities in the area that mimic those of Connecticut locations.

The Firelands were purchased from Indians for about $19,000 and consisted of the lands that would ultimately become Huron and Erie Counties, as well as Ruggles Township in Ashland County, Danbury Township and a portion of what is now Catawba Island Township in Ottawa County.

In 1806, Benajah Wolcott joined a crew of thirteen men hired by Taylor Sherman, a commissioner of the Connecticut Land Company and grandfather of William Tecumseh Sherman, to identify and mark the Firelands. At the time he was contacted about the survey, Wolcott was in New York. Fortunately, he had stayed in contact with Danbury, Connecticut lawyer and acquaintance Epaphroditus W. Bull. Whether Wolcott joined in the survey work itself or simply assisted as a teamster or in some other capacity is not clear. The crew left Danbury with three wagons and eight horses but returned with just four men. The survey took just over one year.

During the survey, apparently, Wolcott made his desire to live in the area known. Wallace B. White wrote, in *The Fire Lands Series Lorain Journal* in 1960, that Almon Ruggles, in his field notes, mentions sighting on "Walcott's button ball" (sycamore) when he ran the traverse of the lake shore in 1808.

Bull held the title to much of the land that currently composes the peninsula separating Sandusky Bay from Lake Erie. At the time of the survey, there were three apple orchards on the peninsula, planted by the handful of French and Indians who lived on the peninsula in 1800. Bull had purchased all the peninsula land east of Meadowbrook, including what is now called Johnson's Island. At the time, it was called Bull's Island. In August 1809, he sold Wolcott 114 acres for a sum of $190, to be paid over three years' time. The contract called for Wolcott to live on the land for at least five years and to build a road along the Sandusky Bay shore. Interestingly, the $190 Wolcott agreed to pay Bull was significantly less than the then-current rate for such land.

The area eventually settled by many former Connecticut residents included much of present-day Erie, Ottawa and Sandusky Counties. Most of the settlers, however, had not suffered losses at British hands in Connecticut but had purchased parcels from land speculators who had gobbled up a large percentage of the half-million acres. Wolcott was one of those settlers, though he appears to have gotten a far better deal than others.

In 1809, after completing the survey work and returning to Connecticut, Wolcott returned to the peninsula, which was still a wilderness of prairie and forest. William W. Williams in *History of the Fire Lands*, published in 1886, gave this account of Wolcott's return to the peninsula:

> *Mr. Wolcott and his family, consisting of his wife, two daughters and one son, and accompanied by two hired men, named Bishop and Osborn, left Connecticut, in a sleigh, February 13, 1809. They arrived in Cleveland in March, but the lake being ice bound, the family was unable to proceed farther, and remained there until about the first of May. Mr. Wolcott, accompanied by Bishop and Osborn, proceeded, to the peninsula by land, to prepare a house for those left in Cleveland, make [a] garden and arrange as far as possible for a permanent home. In May, Mr. Wolcott returned to Cleveland for his family, and the lake being open, secured passage on a small schooner, the* Sally of Cuyahoga, *for their home. A severe storm*

assailed them, while on the vessel, and they narrowly escaped shipwreck, but finally were able to secure safety by running into Black river, where they remained until the weather became settled, when they proceeded on their voyage, arriving in Sandusky bay on the evening of the 8th of May, and the next day landed at what was then known as "Middle Orchard," on the peninsula, near where now stands Fox's dock. Wolcott and his family were the first settlers in Danbury.

Wolcott and his two hired hands raised a log cabin on the Sandusky Bay side of the peninsula, just a few hundred feet from the bay, and began clearing land. The cabin was located very near the stone house that was erected when Wolcott returned to the peninsula after the war.

After the Wolcotts arrived, others followed. Bull, Revolutionary War veteran Ezra Lee and four other men arrived, with their families, during the next two years. The June 1870 *Firelands Pioneer* described early peninsula life: "Up to the time of Hull's surrender [1812], the settlers of Danbury, although suffering some privations and enduring the hardships peculiar to early pioneer life, had prospered and had kept heart. They believed they had some advantages over some new settlers, and had faith in the 'good time coming.'"

Historical accounts indicate the Wolcotts and the handful of other settlers enjoyed non-hostile relations with the Indians who remained in the area at the beginning of the nineteenth century. Wolcott enjoyed a well-documented friendship with Ottawa chief Ogontz, who had been taken in and raised by whites. Ogontz was educated at a Jesuit college in either Montreal or Quebec. He had also been educated as a Catholic priest.

Rebecca Bostwick, who traveled with pioneer families, including the Bulls and Wolcotts in 1811, later wrote about Wolcott and peninsula life:

The first party or gathering we had was to a Christmas dinner at the house of Mr. Peck, a part of which our family occupied with them. Nearly all the people in the settlement were invited and enjoyed it much. Our entertainment consisted of a large swan, ducks and chickens, roasted, including 20 mince pies baked in a spider, together with the best our market afforded for vegetables, etc. After dinner, a dance was proposed. Mr. Wolcott playing the violin, and although the puncheon floor was not as level or as smooth as it might have been, we enjoyed it well.

As the Bulls, Wolcotts, Bostwicks and others were settling into their peninsula frontier, relations between the United States and Britain were

The Marblehead Lighthouse Historical Society volunteers adorn the lighthouse with wreaths and bows every Christmas season. *Author's photo*.

quickly deteriorating. Royal Navy captains began seizing American merchant vessels in order to press American sailors into service on Royal Navy ships. In June 1812, President James Madison signed a declaration of war on Britain. Antiwar protests broke out in Baltimore and other cities. Battles raged on land and sea for several years. Some battles were as far away as Brazil, while others were as close as what is now known as Danbury Township, just a few miles from the site of what would soon become home to the Sandusky Bay Light Station.

Just prior to the War of 1812, Ogontz lived in a shanty just across the Sandusky Bay. Ogontz and Wolcott were said to often visit each other, usually by Wolcott's rowing across the bay. With war near at hand, the British had recruited various Indian warriors in their quest to defeat the Americans. Soon-to-be-conquered lands were promised as payment to Indians for assisting the British. A month after the war declaration, Bull wrote to General Elijah Wadsworth, who commanded the troops of the Western Reserve. The letter reads, in part:

> *The following, very shortly, is our situation: We are on a Peninsula by ourselves, surrounded by water on all sides except on the West where we border on Indian lands. In case of trouble, our own flight must be by water. We have no water craft of consequence to take ourselves off…they might come over in a night, destroy us, and return by way of the Islands to Malden…To live in a state of suspense, of doubt and danger, is dreadful.*

Bull goes on to describe a blockhouse being constructed for the safety of settlers if need be and requested that troops be sent to the peninsula. He tells Wadsworth that about one hundred people live in the area. Just a few months later, the settlers would be gone.

William Hull, a Revolutionary War veteran and later a judge and senator, was governor of Michigan Territory just before the war began. He reluctantly reentered military service at age sixty at the rank of brigadier general and was given control of both regular infantry and militia units from Ohio and Indiana. He briefly attacked Canada after crossing the Detroit River and then retreated. On August 16, 1812, Hull's force numbered almost 2,200 at Fort Detroit, but he was outplayed on a battlefield that saw no battle. British major general Isaac Brock, with a force of just 1,300, used well-placed and well-timed artillery shots and loud, repeated war cries from a force of about 600 Indians to solicit the fort's surrender. The soldiers under Hull's command were so disgusted that they refused to carry out a white surrender flag. Instead, a young boy displayed the flag to the approaching enemy. Hull was subsequently court-martialed and sentenced to death. In the end, President Madison spared his life. Brock's battle report read:

> *Major-General Brock to Sir George Prevost.*
> *Head Quarters Detroit:*
> *August 16, 1812.*
>
> *Sir—I hasten to apprize Your Excellency of the Capture of this very important Post: 2,500 troops have this day surrendered Prisoners of War, and about 25 Pieces of Ordnance have been taken, without the Sacrifice of a drop of British blood; I had not more than 700 troops including Militia, and have about 400 Indians to accomplish this Service. When I detail my good fortune Your Excellency will be astonished. I have been admirably supported by Colonel Procter, the whole of my Staff and I may justly say every individual under my command.*

Wolcott's close alliance with Ogontz has been credited as the reason Wolcott's home was not attacked by Indians and his family remained safe as hostilities between the nations simmered and even after they boiled over. The cabin home that the Wolcotts left behind remained safe even as a bloody battle took place—often called one of the first battles of the War of 1812—just a few hundred yards away.

Even Chief Ogontz decided he could not remain in the area. A *Women's Endeavor* article from March 1908 addressed Ogontz's retreat:

> *The lodge which Ogontz occupied stood near the site of the old Second National Bank on Columbus Avenue, between Water and Market streets. It was a favorite custom of Ogantz to sit down among the hawthorns that line the banks of the bay and look out across its fair waters. It was a charming sight then. It is a charming sight today. A lover and counselor of peace, when the war clouds of 1812 began to threaten, Ogontz, knowing they could not remain neutral, removed with his people to Canada. After the war, he returned and settled on the Maumee River; he often came back to Ogontz Place to visit the home he had loved so much.*

Horace Ramsdell, who had come to the area with his family in 1811, wrote about his experiences in the *Firelands Pioneer* (1870):

When the settlers fled from the Peninsula in 1812, we took some of them down the shore to Vermillion and elsewhere in our boat. After this was done, we took our boat and Capt. Austin's and went back to the Orchards to bring away some hemp. Thompson & Co. of Buffalo had stored there 50 tons of hemp which they had brought from Delaware, Ohio, by way of Fremont; While there, and just as we were leaving, some soldiers landed at the orchards. They were from Huron, and came in a scow to get fruit & etc. They set one man, named Guy, as a sentinel to keep watch while the others gathered apples. He stuck his gun into the ground by the bayonet, and climbed into an apple tree from the fence. As I passed him, going to the boat, I told him he was a pretty guard: if there were any Indians about there, they would steal his gun and shoot him before he knew it. He swore he was not afraid: he could get his gun before the Indian could. We started away with the hemp and left the soldiers there, and Guy still in the tree near the water. I was rowing the boat, and when only a few rods away, as I sat looking toward the orchard, I saw a puff of smoke, heard the report of a gun, and saw the soldiers drop from the trees as though they had all been shot, and throwing their things hither and thither, they made for their boat. Guy fell, shot through the forehead, and it was said that he was shot with the charge in his own gun, by an Indian.

The battle site is marked with an Ohio Historical Marker plaque today. It reads:

The first War of 1812 battle on Ohio soil was fought here when about 60 exhausted citizen soldiers were ambushed by about 130 Indians on September 29. Twenty men held the Indians at bay in a cabin while the main body escaped by boat to Cedar Point. Two days later the defenders were rescued. Forty Indians including several chiefs and 8 Americans were killed in the skirmish, neither a victory nor a defeat for either side.

Shortly after the American general surrendered Detroit to the British, settlers on the peninsula fled east. Boats on Lake Erie that were approaching the peninsula signaled trouble for settlers. The invaders were likely British soldiers or hostile Indians. Bull's wife, Polly, wrote about the experience in the *Firelands Pioneer* in 1859:

During the summer [1812], rumors of war and dread of its actual approach rendered us somewhat disquieted. Some, taking counsel of their fears, left

This historical marker at the location of an Indian/settler skirmish along the banks of Sandusky Bay is just a few hundred feet from the site of Benajah Wolcott's home. *Author's photo.*

the peninsula. It was not, however, until some time in August, when our whole family was suffering with chills and fever, that actual danger seemed to threaten us. One morning, men upon the Lake shore informed us that the boats of the enemy were coming down the Lake, and seemed prepared to land. We supposed the party to consist of hostile Indians. I caught up a woolen sheet upon reception of the news, tore it in two, and hastily throwing these garments around my two youngest children—one about four and the other two years old—consigned them to the care of two of our hired men, while the rest of us made rapid preparations to follow them in flight. A few of our most important articles in housekeeping, we concealed in bush heaps, and then made all the haste to cross the bay, for safety. All the families then upon the peninsula embarked in the same boat, and so we crossed over to Sandusky…After proceeding some distance [to Huron] we reached a creek, which a short time before, as we learned afterwards, our two hired men, carrying my two youngest children, as I have before stated, had crossed in safety, so swollen with rain that we could not follow them. We spent the night in the woods. In the morning, we received intelligence of Hull's surrender, and the disbandment of his forces, and that those who we supposed to be the enemy, were our own troops, on their way home.

The men, of course, were not invaders at all, but merely a group of the American soldiers who had recently been paroled by British forces after Hull's surrender at Fort Detroit the previous month. Polly wrote that a short time later, when the settlers in Huron had learned of Hull's surrender and the true nature of the men in the boats, they returned to the peninsula, gathered their possessions and headed for the relative safety of the East.

The Bull and Wolcott families were among those who chose the safety of eastern settlements, like Vermilion, Huron and Newburgh, a settlement on the Cuyahoga River. Wolcott's wife, Elizabeth, died there. Bull died, too, after evacuating his family from the perceived dangers. After his death, Bull's

The United States brig *Niagara* fires a volley during the Battle of Lake Erie reenactment in September 2013. Perry's victory over the British fleet helped open the Great Lakes, and especially Lake Erie, to American commerce. *Author's photo.*

wife and children returned to a safer, more settled and civilized Connecticut, never to return to the Firelands.

In 1813, Commodore Oliver Hazard Perry defeated a fleet of Royal Navy vessels on Lake Erie, about a dozen miles northeast of the islands in the Western Basin. In a brief, vicious battle on a beautiful September afternoon, Perry and his fleet devastated a formidable enemy. On the back of an envelope, Perry sent a hastily written note to United States general William Henry Harrison:

> *Dear General:*
> *We have met the enemy and they are ours. Two ships, two brigs, one schooner and one sloop.*
> *Yours with great respect and esteem,*
> *O.H. Perry*

The American naval victory signaled a soon-to-come security for American trade and transportation on the Great Lakes and, thus, a bright future for the cities, towns and ports located on the lakes. While the War of 1812 placed America's expansion on hold, it didn't stop the prosperous nation's hunger for growth. Military historian Maurice Matloff wrote in *American Military History*:

> *As a result of the victory, which illustrated successful employment of the principles of offensive and mass, Lake Erie became an American Lake. The Indian confederacy was shattered. The American position on the Detroit frontier was re-established, a portion of Canadian territory was eliminated. There was no further fighting here for the rest of the war.*

Some 185 years later, a local man was walking on the beach at Bay Point, near the lighthouse, during his lunch break from operating heavy equipment. He spied the tip of something sticking out of the sand. After digging for some time, his efforts produced a 59.75-inch musket. It turned out to be a Charleville .69-caliber flintlock. The French weapon was a common one used by the United States in the late 1700s, including during the Revolutionary War. After the local paper reported the find, the man gave a presentation to a history class at the local school. Similar weapons from the same era have been found in the area over the years.

While some speculated that no settlers would return to the peninsula from the east during the 1812–13 winter, at least one family did. On January 10, 1813, John H. Patch wrote a letter in which Benajah Wolcott is mentioned:

Gen Wadsworth informs me that he met Woolcot [sic] at Black River as he was returning home. He [was] with his family and was removing back to the Peninsula. I am very sorry to hear that he has gone back quite so soon, as it is apprehended, and very much feared that he and his family will fall sacrifice to savage barbarity.

After the war ended, according to the *Firelands Pioneer* in 1887, "Mr. Wolcott remained with his family at Newberg until Harrison had driven the British and hostile Indians into Canada, and then he returned to the Peninsula and went to work on his farm, as hopeful as ever." Wolcott and his family returned to the peninsula and resumed their pioneering ways. A historical account printed in the *Firelands Pioneer* in 1870 helps illustrate Wolcott's character:

In 1825 Cleveland had grown to be a smart little burgh, and the Clevelanders thought they would add to their importance, and at the same time fire up their patriotism by celebrating the first fourth of July after the declaration of peace by holding an old-fashioned Independence ball. Everything was at hand but the music. Mr. Wolcott's fame had reached as far as the mouth of the Cuyahoga, and he was at once ordered to put in an appearance on the occasion. He never disobeyed these orders, and at once set about his preparations for the journey, and invited his youngest daughter to share the pleasures of the journey. She, nothing loth to have a little patriotic fun with the Cleveland belles and beaux, gave her best "gown" a few extra touches and was ready. The old man took his violin under his arm and mounted one horse. She mounted another, and riding down to "the meadow" at the east point of the Peninsula, west of Cedar Point, they took a canoe and, swimming their horses behind them across the mouth of the Bay, over to the Point, and then, mounting their horses, again took the trail through the woods, via Huron, for Cleveland, swimming the streams as they came to them, and making the best of their way in true pioneer style. As the daughter finished the story, the old lady added, with a twinkle of the eye, "The girls did not wear hoops in my time. What would 'the belle of the season' say in our time of a horse-back ride of seventy miles through an unbroken forest, along an Indian trail to attend a ball?"

Years later, Joseph Root published a piece in the *Firelands Pioneer* in which he described the life of Wolcott and his family as one of extreme privation. Root also described Wolcott in flattering terms: "He was an honest, industrious and cheerful man; tried to be happy himself and to make others happy. He sometimes played on the violin, and, as I thought, well."

The *Clarion*, in 1827, published a detailed review of Sandusky commerce during the previous five years. In 1822, a year after the Sandusky Bay Light Station (as it was known until 1870) was erected, the keeper logged 178 lake arrivals. In subsequent years, there were 190, 254, 286 and, in 1826, 355 arrivals.

In 1818, the lake saw its first steamship arrive, *Walk-in-the-Water*. The 138-foot vessel boasted a pair of masts with three sails and a large paddlewheel. Just three years later, in October 1821, *Walk-in-the-Water* was caught in a storm and washed ashore on a beach near the lighthouse in Buffalo. Fortunately, all eighteen passengers and the crew were saved.

As trade grew, the need for lighthouses to safeguard ships on the lakes became dire, especially in the Sandusky area, a favored port among Great Lakes captains. Hewson L. Peeke, author of *The Centennial History of Erie County, Ohio*, wrote in 1925, "From the earliest days of lake navigation, Sandusky harbor has been considered the best of the chain of lakes. Practically landlocked, it offers a safe haven in time of storm and gives anchorage room for more vessels than any other harbor on the inland seas."

In 1818, the first two Great Lakes lighthouses were built, both on Lake Erie. One was constructed at Buffalo, New York, and another at Presque Isle, Pennsylvania. Interestingly, the lantern from Presque Isle (also known as Erie Land Lighthouse or Erie Main Light), the lake's second lighthouse, was eventually dismantled and transferred to the lake's third lighthouse almost a century later, where it still remains in service.

A lighthouse in the Western Basin would arrive none too soon. A fixed navigation beacon was much needed by the time the construction of the Sandusky Bay Light Station began. Major Joseph Delafield, working on the first survey of the Canadian boundary line from St. Regis to Lake of the Woods, in 1820, wrote in his personal journal on June 12:

> *At day light we leave the steam boat under Cunningham Island [Kelleys Island] and take passage in a small schooner for Sandusky. A cabin crowded with emigrants is less intolerable than to brace the storm on deck. To add to our miseries the vessel is forced upon the bar about two miles from the landing. Finding their endeavors to get her off fruitless, I embark with Mrs. Camp, Miss Robertson & Mr. Ainslie in the small boat for Sandusky.*

His entry makes a strong case for the establishment of a beacon to assist captains sailing into and out of Sandusky. The year before, on March 1, 1819, just two days before adjourning, the Fifteenth Congress passed measures approving the construction of a light station somewhere on Lake Erie. The measure approved lighthouses, beacons and buoys in Boston, Buzzard and Chesapeake Bays and on Lakes Ontario and Erie. When Congress approved the new Lake Erie lighthouse, there were fewer than seventy residents of Danbury Township.

The bill authorized the creation of other navigational aids on many of the nation's other waterways, too.

During proceedings of the new Sixteenth Congress, Connecticut representative James Stevens suggested that "the committee on Transportation be asked to report on the feasibility of erecting a lighthouse on the south shore of Lake Erie, at or near the confluence of its waters with those of Sandusky Bay."

But penny-pinching Virginia representative John Randolph balked at the possible expenditure:

> *The moneys of the United States are being scattered from Passamaquoddy to Yellowstone, from Chicago to Mobile. We are like the Georgia and Virginia planters, cotton being at fifty cents and tobacco thirty dollars. "Do you want a toothpick? Take a hundred dollars. Do you want a toothbrush? Take a hundred dollars"…Even a blind man can see the dilapidation of public funds. But I would as soon attempt to be heard across the Potomac in the face of a northwester as to be heard here.*

On May 15, 1820, Congress set aside funds for the project "out of moneys in the treasury not otherwise appropriated, for a lighthouse to be built between the mouth of the Grand River in the State of Ohio and the Detroit River in the Territory of Michigan, $5,000."

While Stevens's support for such a lighthouse was based on the practical needs of Lake Erie navigation, it was also based, at least in part, on business. He was the attorney for Epaphraditus Bull's estate, which still held land on the Marblehead Peninsula. At that time, it was called Rocky Point. Connecticut native James Kilbourne—an Episcopal minister, former congressman and surveyor who helped found the cities of Worthington, Bucyrus and Sandusky—assisted officials in locating a suitable site for the new lighthouse. Charles Frohman, in *Sandusky's Yesterdays*, explained: "James Kilbourn, one of the proprietors of Sandusky, went with U.S. Commissioner Col. Foster to fix the site for a lighthouse. He showed him Cape Sandy at the entrance to Sandusky Harbor, and Rocky Point at the end of the Marblehead Peninsula. The latter was chosen."

On August 21, 1821, the heirs of Epaphroditus Bull—his children, Epaphras W., Edward and Emily—through their guardian Polly Bull, sold the land situated at what was then called Rocky Point to the United States government. The parcel, recorded in the deed records of what was then Huron County, was purchased for $89.50 per acre. The original survey is recorded as follows:

> *Beginning at a post on the shore of Lake Erie at a place called Rocky Point at the easterly extremity of the peninsula, North of Sandusky Bay, about three miles from the entrance of said Bay, thence running North fifty nine degrees west four chains to an ash tree, thence north sixty five degrees west three chains eighty seven and a half links along the shore of the lake to an ash, thence south twenty two degrees West four chains to a post, thence south sixty two degrees East, seven chains and seventy five links to a post on the shore of the lake, thence north twenty two degrees east four chains to the place of beginning, containing by estimation three acres and sixteen perches more or less, bounded south eastwardly and north eastwardly by Lake Erie.*

The total cost of the land was $277.45. Decades later, in 1873, another $100.00 was spent to purchase a twenty- by five-hundred-foot easement from the road that wound around the peninsula to the lighthouse parcel.

The construction contract was awarded to Sandusky builder Stephen Woolverton, who would go on to construct many lighthouses and associated structures for the United States government. But records indicate he was not involved directly in the construction labor. Instead, it was subcontracted to a local stonemason. That mason, William Kelly, was born in Ireland in 1779 and was a Sandusky resident at the time of construction. Despite a colorful and adventurous early life, after settling in Sandusky, Kelly built many significant homes and structures. A number of his buildings stand today.

While in Ireland, Kelly took part in violent anti-Catholic clashes. He was so involved in the political and religious strife that his wife sewed a steel plate in his shirt, protecting his heart, in case he was shot. After he was shot, he was imprisoned. Due to his affiliation with the Masonic Order in England, his wife appealed to Kelly's fraternal brothers, who eventually secured his release. Shortly after, Kelly left for the United States, at the century's dawn.

After first settling in Troy, New York, Kelly and his second wife settled in Sandusky in 1816. He was the city's first stonemason. Kelly also entered

This undated image is likely one of the earliest taken of the Sandusky Bay Light Station. *Courtesy of the Ottawa County Historical Museum.*

business with a partner in a store and pharmacy. While he built dozens of structures, his most enduring and popular legacy is the Marblehead Lighthouse. Amazingly, the construction itself took just eight weeks, primarily involving Kelly, his teenage son John and two helpers. The contract for construction was detailed and exact in its requirements:

August 16, 1821

Articles of Agreement made and entered into on the sixteenth day of August, in the year of our Lord One thousand eight hundred and twenty one, between Thomas Forster, Collector of the Customs at Erie, in the State of Pennsylvania, on behalf of the United States, of the one part, and Stephen Woolverton, of Erie, in said state of the other part, witneyseth [sic], that the said Stephen Woolverton on his part, agrees and engages to build a light house, dwelling house and well, on the peninsula which forms the western shore of the entrance into Sandusky Bay, in the State of Ohio, of the following materials dimensions and description.

The tower to be round, built of stone. The foundation to be sunk as deep as may be necessary to make the whole fabric secure. To be laid in good lime mortar. The height of the tower to be fifty five feet from the surface of the ground. The diameter of the base to be twenty five feet and that of the top to be twelve feet. The thickness of the walls at the base to be five feet, and to be uniformly graduated to two feet at the top. The top to be arched, on which is to be laid a deck of granite stone, fourteen and a half feet in diameter, five inches thick, the points filled in with lead; one side of which to be a scuttle, twenty four by forty inches, to enter the lantern. The scuttle door an iron frame covered with copper. The outside wall is to be well pointed and whitewashed twice over. There are to be six windows in the tower, of twelve lights each, each of ten by eight glass, in strong frames, and a door five feet by three feet, made of double inch boards crop nailed, with substantial hinges, lock and latch. The ground floor to be paced with brick or stone. A sufficient number of circular stairs to lead from the ground floor to within six feet of the lantern connected by a center post, guarded by a good hand railing. The stairs, runners and floors of each story to be made of good pine clear of sap, the stairs and floors to be two inch plank planed. From the top of the stairs to the entrance of the scuttle to be an iron ladder, with steps two and a half inches square. On the top of the tower to be an iron lantern of an octagon form. The posts to be two inches square to run down five feet into the stone work and secured with anchors. The height and diameter of the lanterns to be sufficient to admit an iron sash in each octagon, to contain twenty one lights of fourteen by twelve glass, the lower tier to be filled with copper; the rabbits of the sashes to be three quarters of an inch deep, and glazed with double glass from the Boston Manufactory. In one of the octagons to be an iron framed door covered with copper, four feet by two in the clear, to fit tight in the rabbits with a strong turned button. The top to be a dome formed by sixteen iron rafters concentrating in an iron hoop,

This undated photo was taken from shore on the western side of the lighthouse. *Courtesy of the Ottawa County Historical Museum.*

five inches wide and nine inches diameter, covered with copper, thirty two ounces to the square foot, which is to come down and wick into the piece that forms the top of the sash, which is to be three inches wide. On the dome to be a traversing ventilator two and a half feet long and fifteen inches diameter, on which is to be secured a vane three feet long and twenty inches wide. The ventilator and vane to be framed with iron and covered with copper, and painted black. Around the lantern to be an iron railing, two posts of which to be one and three eights of an inch square connected by three railings three quarters of an inch squared, the upper one to be four feet from the deck. The lantern and wood work of the tower to be painted twice over with white lead, except the dome, which is to be black. The light house to be furnished with one completed electrical conductor three quarters of an inch in diameter, with points.

Like the specifications for the tower, detailed instructions were laid out for the keeper's house:

The dwelling house to be built of stone, thirty four feet by twenty, one story eight feet on the clear, the foundation of the walls to be sunk as deep as is necessary to make the house secure, and laid in lime mortar. The walls to be one foot thick. The roof to be rectangular. The house to be divided into two rooms, with a chimney in the middle, and an entry six feet wide in front of the chimney. A fire place in each room and closets back of the chimney. Stairs to lead from the entry into the chambers, which are to be partitioned off and lathed and plastered and double floored, well nailed. The inside wall and ceiling to be lathed and plastered. Three windows in each room, each to contain sixteen lights, ten by eight glass and each of the same size in each chamber. All the timber to be good heart pine, and the boards to be well seasoned. The roof to be shingled with good pine shingles. The doors to be all four paneled, to have good hinges and thumb latches. The outside door to have a good lock. Attached to the house to be a kitchen fourteen feet by twelve, the walls stone same as the house, double floor; the inside walls and ceiling lathed and plastered, two windows, twelve lights each, ten by eight, two doors four paneled, one to lead into the house and the other outside; the doors to have good hinges and thumb latches. A chimney with an iron crane, trammel and hooks. On one side of the chimney, an oven of a middling size with an iron door, on the other side a sink, with a gutter to lead through the stone wall. The roof to be covered the same as the house, with spouts to lead off the water, an outhouse five feet by four, boarded and shingled. All the woodwork, inside and out, to be painted twice over. A well to be sunk sufficiently deep to procure good waters, at a convenient distance from the lighthouse, to be stoned and furnished with a curb, windlass and an iron chain, and a strong iron hooped bucket. And the said Stephen Woolverton further agrees and engages to fix up the said lighthouse within one month after it shall be built, with fifteen patent lamps and fifteen nine inch reflectors, and nine inch lenses, ten tin butts for keeping the oil, and all the necessary apparatus in the same manner as the light house in the United States have been fitted up by Winslow Lewis, viz; Ten wooden horses, two spare lamps, one lantern, canister and trivet, two three gallon canisters, one tin torch, one oil carrier, six wick forming, two tube cleaners, one hand lantern, two files, two pair scissors, one tub box, one wick box, one hacking knife and putty knife, two buff skins, one tub (30 lb) whiting, two oil strainers, one oil feeder. In consideration whereof the said Thomas Forster for and on behalf of the United States, as aforesaid, engages to pay the said Stephen Woolverton for doing and performing the work, and finding, the sum of six thousand five hundred and twenty dollars in the following manner, Viz; Two thousand dollars when the contract and bond for the faithful performance thereof shall be executed by the said Woolverton, two thousand dollars when the light house shall be carried up to the height of thirty feet, and the remaining sum of two thousand five hundred and twenty dollars when the whole work shall be completed and approved.

It is hereby provided that no member of Congress shall be admitted to any share or part of this contract of agreement, or to any benefit to arise thereupon.

Signed by Stephen Woolverton
Tho. Forster.
Witnessed by E. Freeman and Sam L. Forster.

Both the lighthouse and the keeper's house were constructed of limestone. Evidence of a small quarry operation nearby exists, but no direct evidence indicates exactly where the limestone for the tower and the keeper's house came from. The small quarry is likely the site and lies about seven hundred feet from the lighthouse in a now-wooded area near the roadway. Evidence suggests the stone used to build Wolcott's home was also quarried on-site.

What is certain is that the construction of both was satisfactory to government officials, evidenced by the 1822 inspection report by Thomas Forster:

I certify that I have carefully and particularly inspected and examined the light house, dwelling house, kitchen, well, erected and made by Stephen Woolverton, near Sandusky Bay, in the State of Ohio, under the annexed contract, and find they are of the dimensions and composed of the materials mentioned in said contract, that the workmanship in every respect is good and well put together and that all the stipulations in this contract are complete with excepting the construction of the lighting apparatus, which differs from that in the contract by the interposition of Winslow Lewis Esq. who has furnished them. I further certify that I am convinced, and it is the opinion of every person of knowledge who has seen the light, that it answers a much better purpose than if lighted as mentioned in the contract.

Signed at Erie, PA July 15, 1822 by Tho. Forster, Superintendent.

The total cost of the lighthouse, keeper's house, well and outbuildings came to $6,520. Woolverton was paid $2,000 upfront, $2,000 when the height of the tower reached thirty feet and the remaining $2,520 after the projects were inspected and approved. Kelly billed forty and a half days at $1.50 each, while two helpers billed days at 87.5 cents per day.

Interestingly, the contract for the construction of the lighthouse and keeper's house included a corruption clause, as did many of the government's contracts at the time, specifying that "no member of Congress shall be

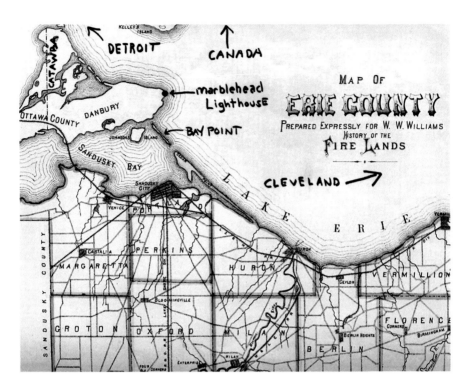

An 1896 Erie County Township map. *Courtesy of the Sandusky Public Library.*

admitted to any share or part of this contract of agreement, or to any benefit to arise thereupon."

While Wolcott and some other families returned to the peninsula after the war, Epaphroditus Bull, Elizabeth Wolcott and another settler died from fever in autumn 1812. It is reported that Benajah Wolcott and others, including the Bull children, had all suffered it but recovered. Bull's wife and children never returned to the peninsula but returned east to Connecticut.

After returning to the area and later receiving his pension, Wolcott married Rachel Miller in Sandusky, just a few months before being appointed keeper.

Chapter 3

THE EARLY YEARS AND
THE FIRST KEEPER

President James Monroe appointed Wolcott keeper of the newly constructed lighthouse on June 24, 1822. Prior to the appointment, a number of area residents had signed a petition expressing confidence in Wolcott's ability to keep the lighthouse in operation. To businessmen in Sandusky, safe navigation was an important component to the future of Lake Erie and Great Lakes trade.

Lyman Farwall, Peter Ferry, Eleutheros Cooke, Cyrus W. Marsh and other leading figures in the region signed an August 1821 letter addressed to Secretary of the Treasury William W. Crawford. A second, undated letter—signed by sixteen individuals, who described themselves as "gentlemen of the first and highest Standing in Society"—was sent to President James Monroe. If the petition on Wolcott's behalf is any indication, he most certainly was in good standing with folks in Sandusky (then called Portland) and elsewhere in the region:

And your petitioners, would further represent in Support of the just Claims of Mr. Wolcott to the appointment aforesaid, that he faithfully and honorably served in his Country during Six Years…of the Revolutionary War; that during 15 years past, he has resided on the Peninsula within one half mile of the Site fixed upon for the erection of the Said light house, during which, he sustained the hardships and Struggled the dangers and privations incident to the Settlement of a new and frontier County: that during the late war, he was driven by the British and Indians from his possessions on the peninsula—plundered of all the hard earnings of his industry for a long series of years; and thrown upon the world, at an advanced age, almost pennyless and destitute; that he now, by the assistance of his pension, and the exertion of his industry, Struggles hard to support himself and family.

And your petitioners, would further represent that Mr. Wolcott is now about 59 years of age, that, though he is in somewhat enfeebled by the fatigues, while he has been destined to encounter and thereby rendered unable to Sustain the heat and burden of hard labor, yet he is still, active in busying industry & Steady in his habits; that his is a man of unblemished Character and incorruptible integrity, and in the Opinions of your Petitioners every way qualified to discharge all the duties of Superintendent of said Light house. And should he be appointed, they have no doubt but he will discharge them with the utmost vigilance, premptitude and fidelity.

While his first official day on the job was June 24, 1822, Wolcott seems to have taken up his duties a bit earlier—and impressed at least one person. A journal entry made by Methodist minister David Marks on June 17 sheds a kind light on Wolcott. Marks was more or less stranded at the lighthouse for a short time, at least a week or two earlier:

The wind and storm abated. Our voyage having been longer than we expected, and the wind being still contrary, the captain of the vessel, notwithstanding his engagement, refused to take me to Portland [Sandusky], and after receiving my last money for the passage, he set me with four others on the peninsula west of Sandusky bay and six miles opposite Portland. Here was a lighthouse, and besides the man who kept it there were no inhabitants in that part of the peninsula. It was now after sun-set, and during the last forty hours I had eaten but one meal, which was given me by the captain of the vessel. The man who kept the lighthouse had but little provisions with him, having been disappointed of an expected recruit in consequence of the unfavorable wind. So without food I lay down on the floor and closed my eyes to sleep, hoping to forget my hunger.

Marks went on to write that Wolcott, taking full consideration that a preacher had traveled far from home to spread the gospel, awoke him later, offering half a pint of milk and a cracker. Marks's eloquent praise was not confined to Wolcott:

Next morning the sun rose with splendor and I walked out to view the surrounding scenery...Going into the top of the light-house [sic] I looked eastward, and though my hunger was oppressive, and I could neither see my native land, nor any place where I had formerly traveled, yet I found Christ to be precious, and his love filled my soul.

Marks wouldn't have known it at the time, but surely he was one of the very first of millions to visit the lighthouse in the coming centuries and likely one of the first visitors to climb the new pine steps to the top of the lighthouse. Later that day, he and his fellow travelers went into the woods and shot a fawn, which they cooked and ate with no seasoning, not even salt. They wandered, he wrote, enthralled at a nearby meadow with tall grasses, and were struck by the beauty of the peninsula and all it featured.

Wolcott was given a salary of $350 per year. His family was afforded the use of the home, constructed next to the lighthouse, which included a well, a barn and all the associated necessities. The same year he was appointed, Wolcott also had built a home about two miles southwest of the lighthouse, very near the site of the battle a decade earlier. William Kelly, who had completed the Marblehead Lighthouse the previous year, also constructed Wolcott's limestone home.

Four years earlier, Congress had created a pension system for needy veterans of the Revolutionary War. The March 1818 law offered Wolcott a financial opportunity, and he applied the very next month. He was notified in October 1819 that his name was among those placed on a pension roll, but it is likely he never received benefits, because more than a year later, in 1820, he appeared in Huron Court of Common Pleas in Norwalk, Ohio, to plead his case for a service pension. Wolcott listed his military service, including the names of commanders he served under. He then declared both his financial need and that he had not entrusted any property or valuables to anyone else. Following that, Wolcott described his ill health, indicating that he suffered from "rheumatism and infirmities" and that his fifteen-year-old son couldn't work "in consequence of ill health occasioned by a wound on his head." Wolcott was, eventually, approved for a pension prior to his appointment as keeper.

Until 1820, the Lighthouse Board did not require lighthouse keepers to maintain a log of activities, events and occurrences at their stations. But by the time Wolcott's new station was illuminated, the logs were standard. Each day, the keeper wrote a line or brief note in the logbook, conveying information about the day's activities or events. Those entries, over the decades, have varied from keeper to keeper. The entries were often as simple at one or two words. Other times, they were a paragraph, describing a shipwreck, an inspection, a visit, a storm or anything else noteworthy. On some days, keepers made no notations in the logbook. The logs that Wolcott and most other keepers maintained have, unfortunately, been lost to the years.

Few records remain of the years Benajah Wolcott spent tending the station. Merlin Wolcott, a librarian and amateur historian, was a prolific writer on the topic of the Marblehead Lighthouse, the first Marblehead Life-Saving Station and Wolcott's home on Bayshore Road. He is also a descendant of Benajah. In an *Inland Seas* article in 1954, Merlin Wolcott wrote:

> *Benajah's home on the Bay Shore, near the monument marking the place of the Battle of the Peninsula, was completed in 1822. The year is carved on the stone step at the front entrance. My impression is that Benajah built the house himself for his new bride…It seems doubtful the Federal Government would have built the lighthouse keeper's house on private property on Benajah's farm that is some distance from the Lighthouse. In a certificate of acceptance of the Federal property in his possession, Benajah signed for "Possession of three acres of land at Rocky Point on the Shore of Lake Erie, west of the entrance into Sandusky Bay in Huron County of Ohio—a Lighthouse, Dwelling house, Kitchen and necessary outhouse thereon erected, finished and in complete order, with the windows glazed in each, with good well water, water bucket, chain and krib."*
> —*Signed in the presence of Truman Pettibone and Stephen Woolverton.*

Wolcott's life, and that of his family, most certainly improved after his pension award and his appointment as keeper. Wolcott began a friendly relationship with a Sandusky merchant a few years after the lighthouse went into operation, which helped him secure some items that were considered luxuries on the American pioneer front.

The lighthouse's first illumination was attained through the installation of thirteen "patent lamps" fitted with reflectors. The system was designed, in part, in 1781 when Swiss physicist and chemist Aimé Argand designed a new single-wick lamp that emitted about the same amount of light as seven candles.

At the time, Argand's lamps were state of the art, featuring cylindrical wicks and chimneys. His design included wicks surrounded by a round glass chimney, which drew oxygen upward through and around the fuel-soaked wick. This created a flame far more intense than had previously been

The lighthouse and its fuel tank, undated. *Courtesy of the Ottawa County Historical Museum.*

achieved. The lamps were fueled with whale oil, and each was equipped with a reflector to maximize its brightness.

While H.L. Reynaud, director of the French Lighthouse Service, credited Argand with the first proposal of utilizing reflectors, such apparatus in the United States is most often credited to Winslow Lewis. The Massachusetts sea captain patented the Binnacle Illuminator in 1808. Lewis created it using an Argand-style lamp and a series of parabolic reflectors that could illuminate both the binnacle (an above-deck box or stand where a ship's compass is located) and a space below deck. The *New England Palladium* reported Lewis's Binnacle Illuminator took just "one half the oil the Binnacle alone previously used."

During the same time, Lewis began experimenting with convex lenses, which he eventually sold as "patent illuminators, or sky lights for shipping." The glass lenses were installed on ships' decking and provided a magnified light to below-deck spaces. The lighthouse lamp system he would become known for was created when he combined the convex lenses with the Argand-style lamps and parabolic reflectors.

Lewis's system included reflectors made of copper with a silver plating. The plating was often inadvertently removed during the cleaning process, and light keepers reported the assemblies were apt to soot up quickly. The use of Lewis's lamp systems was also labor intensive. Wicks had to be trimmed and changed out frequently. Keepers had to constantly maintain clean chimneys, reflectors and windows in lighthouses. But Lewis's lamp systems outperformed contemporaneous lamps and used far less fuel. The *Balance and State Journal* reported, in 1811, that after Lewis's system was used in Boston Lighthouse, the distance of illumination was greater and the system was more economic. "The old lamps were horribly inefficient, requiring thirty-one gallons of whale oil per week. The new cleaner-burning lamps needed only nine."

In 1812, Lewis sold the patent to his lighting system to the United States government and also received a contract to refit the nation's forty-nine existing lighthouses with his system. In addition, Congress appropriated $60,000 for the refitting and for Lewis's maintaining of the nation's lights for seven years.

While Lewis supplied and maintained the lamp systems for American lighthouses for decades, the affiliation brought controversy later. Around the same time Lewis was developing his system, across the Atlantic, the French were working on a system that proved far better than Lewis's in every way except initial cost. Despite the vast differences, Lewis's inferior design and products remained in American lighthouses for years to come.

Winslow Lewis developed a close relationship with Stephen Pleasonton. That close working relationship appeared to cloud Pleasonton's judgment for several decades. In fact, Lewis held contracts for building lighthouses and provided supplies and lamp systems for many of the government's

The Buffalo depot was the site of a workshop that worked on Fresnel lenses and other supplies for Great Lakes lighthouses, including the Marblehead Lighthouse. *Courtesy of the National Archives.*

lighthouses despite doubt cast on his roles. His influence was wide ranging, from technical and engineering issues to keepers' salaries.

In a letter Lewis wrote to Commissioner of the Revenue Samuel Smith in September 1816, six years before the Sandusky Bay Light Station was first illuminated, he made recommendations about lighthouse keepers' salaries. After visiting every lighthouse in operation in the United States, Lewis sent Smith a list, including notes on the pros and cons of subsistence at each location. The letter is evidence of the great power that Lewis wielded in the operations of the nation's navigation systems. It offers a glimpse as to why his lamp systems were favored for decades over the superior Fresnel lenses, which were soon widely available. In the letter, Lewis gives specific reasons salaries for certain locations should be set at certain amounts:

> *Race Point $300. Situated on the extremity of Cape Cod, has no land for cultivation nor wood, but has the advantage of a good fishery in the summer.*
>
> *Bald Head $400. The site for this new lighthouse is in an area of nine acres which will afford a garden and keep a cow. Wood convenient without*

expense. His present salary is $425. I think it ought to be put on the same footing as Charleston. $400 dollars.

Interestingly, in a table with the evaluations, Lewis listed his proposed salaries, which included a raise from $300 to $350 for Race Point and indicated the Bald Head keeper's salary was currently $400 and should remain so, despite the text of his letter, which indicated the salary was currently $425. For some reason, there are multiple contradictions in his lighthouse salary notes.

Lewis's influence in the operation of the nation's lighthouses continued, much to the detriment of shipping and commerce. It also meant that keepers on the Danbury Peninsula spent decades needlessly cleaning, polishing and fueling Lewis lamps, while European nations adopted the brighter, cleaner, easier-to-operate Fresnel lenses.

As the Marblehead Lighthouse was being constructed on Lake Erie, a French physicist was experimenting with a new lens system that would capture, intensify and optimize light far beyond what Lewis's or any other reflector designs were capable of. Augustin Fresnel's revolutionary lens design would capture up to 83 percent of a flame's illumination.

Prior to Fresnel's work, whale-oil lamps utilizing reflectors, such as the Argand and Lewis lamps, lost up to 40 percent of their light. Before that, the simple optics in lighthouses consisted solely of whale oil lamps placed in the lantern atop towers. This early method offered mariners just about 3 percent of the light produced.

The French government assigned Fresnel to work with Claude Mathieu to make improvements to lighthouse illumination. In 1821, Fresnel created a glass bull's-eye panel made with ringed segments. Refinements made shortly after that included turning the bull's-eye design into a curved lens.

Fresnel's creation surrounded a flame, 360 degrees, with concentric rings of glass. The innovation in Fresnel's design was that glass prisms took light from inside and then redirected it by bending and redirecting the beams through one space. This created an intense, focused beam that could be viewed from the water at distances up to twenty miles.

The term "Fresnel lens" quickly became a generic term for the barrel-shaped dioptric lenses, complemented above and below, with multiple catadioptric prisms. By rotating the optics in conjunction with installation of bull's-eye panels along the circumference of the units, a large number of flashing patterns could be created. These patterns proved valuable when multiple lighthouses were located along a single stretch of coastline. Furthermore, colored glass panels in front of the bull's-eye panels transformed a single lens into a beacon that flashed both a pattern and a color or color sequence.

Eventually, Fresnel's lenses were "ordered," or classified, based on the design and manufacturing sophistication and ranging in sizes from first order, with a focal length of thirty-six inches and a complete assembly of about twelve feet tall, to a sixth order, with a focal length of six inches and a complete assembly of about two feet tall. While most Fresnel lenses were manufactured in France, and at companies in the metropolitan Paris area specifically, some were manufactured in Germany, England and the United States. The Corning Company manufactured small Fresnel-style optics units for use on buoys.

Although Fresnel's innovative design was quickly adopted at lighthouses around the globe, except for the United States, he did not live to see its full dominance. Augustin Fresnel died in 1827. His brother and close assistant, Leonor, took over the business immediately.

But the illumination source on the rocky limestone point at Marblehead remained the same, as did all United States lighthouses, for decades. It was not until the middle of the nineteenth century that Fresnel lenses began replacing inferior Lewis lamp systems. By 1860, all beacons and lighthouses had been fitted with Fresnel lenses, including the Sandusky Bay Light Station.

The expanding United States population demanded more whale oil and other whale products. This sent the price of sperm whale oil—the best quality oil for use in lighting—skyrocketing. Other whale products rose steeply in price as well. From the earliest days, sperm whale oil had been considered the premium fuel for lighthouse lamps. An 1827 contract between New York merchant Zeus Coffin and Stephen Pleasonton was typical of government purchases of top-quality lamp oil, including the Congressional clause at the end:

1st The party of the second part shall furnish and deliver to such person or persons as shall be appointed by the Fifth Auditor of the Treasury and acting Commissioner of the Revenue, to receive the same, forty thousand one hundred and eighty eight gallons of best strained spermaceti oil, and fourteen thousand eight hundred and twenty gallons of best winter strained head matter, in good iron-bound casks, with four additional wooden hoops, of sizes not exceeding sixty gallons.

2nd That the whole of the oil shall be delivered at Nantucket the 1st day of April next, or previous thereto, and shall be previously inspected and approved by the person or persons appointed to receive the same.

3rd That the party of the first part shall pay or allow in settlement to the part of the second part sixty five cents for every gallon of strained spermaceti oil and winter perfused oil from head matter which shall be delivered by the party of the second part, together with an allowance of two dollars per ton for iron-binding with the four additional wooden hoops.

4th That in case of failure or delinquency in the quantity of oil contracted to be delivered by the party of the second part, within the period, at the place, and to the person appointed to receive the same, as mentioned in the first and second artifacts, the party of the first part shall have power to supply the deficiency by purchase, at the risk and on account of the party of the second part.

It is hereby provided that no members of Congress shall be admitted to any share or part of this contract of agreement, or to any benefit to arise thereupon.

The rising demand for whale products kept prices trending upward and meant a healthy trade in the North Atlantic industry, where most of the world's whaling took place. The demand to produce the whales that provided the oils was great. The labor-intensive processes that created sperm whale oil meant the United States Lighthouse Establishment paid dearly to keep lighthouses supplied with oil. Richard C. Kugler described the way lamp fuel was manufactured in *The Whale Oil Trade*:

On delivery, it [head matter] would be heated in a large copper vat to liquefy the sludge-like substance and remove impurities and water. The now-fluid mixture of oil and spermaceti would be drawn off and stored in casks in the shed, where winter cold would congeal and granulate it.

A spongey and viscous mass, it would next be shoveled into strong woolen bags and placed in the most difficult to acquire of all the instruments involved, a large screw press. In this slack press, as it were known, pressure would be applied, forcing from the bag an initial quantity of oil, reading for marketing as an illuminant of lamps at the highest of all oil prices.

In 1833, the American whale fleet included about 392 vessels. By 1846, there were more than 730. This number composed almost 80 percent of the world's whaling fleet, producing more than 10 million gallons of oil annually. While oil prices varied year-to-year, the product eventually became too expensive for use in lighthouses. Between 1831 and 1866, whale oil ranged from 30.5 cents a gallon to $1.92. The average price from 1845 to 1855 was about $1.77 per gallon.

Those prices, along with increasing demand, led lighthouse officials to seek better illuminating fuels. The process of seeking cheaper fuel alternatives was a steady thrust. In fact, as early as 1807, then Secretary of the Treasury Albert Gallatin corresponded with the owners of the merchant vessel *Corlomonde* on the possible procurement of five thousand gallons of "earth oil." Apparently, Gallatin at least theoretically considered "earth oil" the "best article known for burning in lighthouses, making a very strong, clear and bright flame, emitting at the same time a great volume of smoak [*sic*]." Likely, though, the volume of smoke produced by such fuel made the use of it and associated products impractical for lighthouses.

Relief came in the form of rapeseed oil, also known as Colza oil, for about a decade. The nation's farmers failed to grow enough of the nonnative wild cabbage to meet the supply needs. This led the Lighthouse Service to turn to inexpensive, easily obtainable lard. While lard was cost effective and widely available, it tended to congeal when cool and so had to be kept warm so it stayed in a liquid state.

As whale oil supplies dwindled and prices rose, a new source of cheaper, efficient lighting fuel was being developed. The first commercially operated oil well in the United States was sunk in Venango County, Pennsylvania, in 1859. Although that particular well was profitable for just a few years, it ushered in the oil boom and the age of a cheaper, more plentiful illumination source: kerosene.

The discovery of oil and the development of kerosene ushered out lard as a fuel source. Between 1841 and 1885, when kerosene was widely adopted, many experiments were conducted at lighthouses, buoys and beacons. Rosin gases, various petroleum-based products, magnesium combustion products and oil gas had been examined and tested. But by 1877, kerosene was a principal fuel, and by 1885, it was used in almost all American lighthouses.

In August 1832, Wolcott took ill and died suddenly, reportedly of cholera. He was sixty-eight. Historical accounts indicate the disease swept into Sandusky after an elderly woman, apparently infected, came ashore and died before dawn the next day. She had arrived on a schooner from Buffalo. The ship's captain died as well, and the disease quickly spread, soon reaching the peninsula and taking many lives. The condemned ship came close to being burned after it was towed two miles out into Sandusky Bay. The owner, a Sandusky businessman, successfully lobbied to keep it from being destroyed, and the order was subsequently revoked.

Wolcott was reported to have contracted cholera from a body that had washed ashore near the lighthouse. It was common practice for Wolcott and

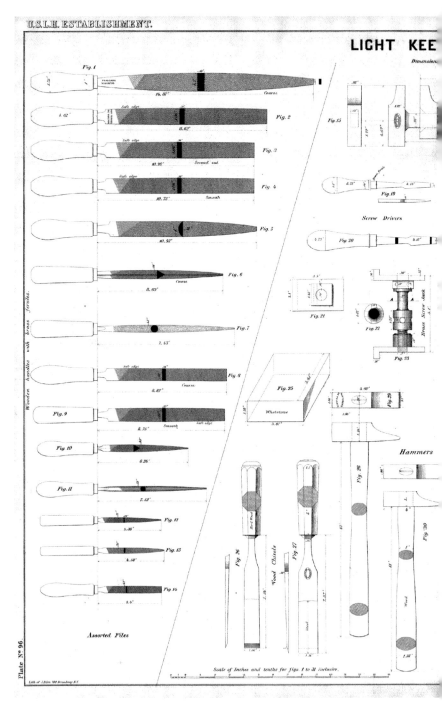

These United States Lighthouse Service drawings illustrate the myriad tools and devices utilized by light keepers. *Courtesy of the National Archives.*

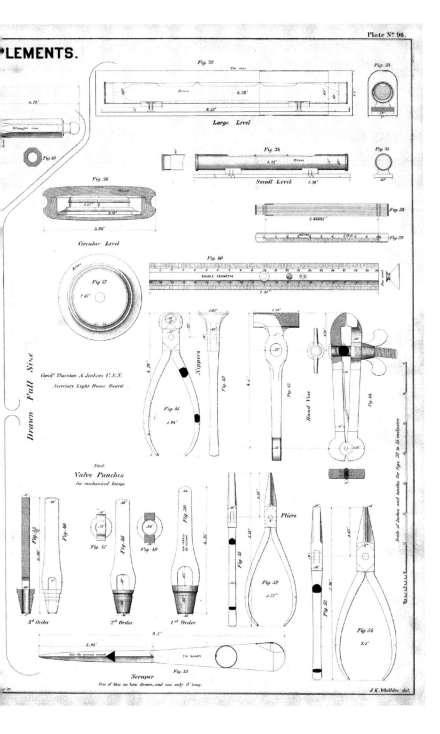

Plate Nº 96.

'LEMENTS.

Fig. 32

Large Level

Fig. 33

Fig. 34

Small Level

Fig. 35

Fig. 36

Circular Level

Fig. 37

Fig. 38

Fig. 39

Fig. 40

DOUBLE DÉCIMÈTRE

Drawn Full Size

Comdr Thornton A. Jenkins U.S.N.
Secretary Light House Board

Fig. 41

Nippers

Fig. 42

Fig. 43

Hand Vice

Fig. 44

Steel
Valve Punches
for mechanical lamps

Scale of Inches and tenths for figs. 32 to 55 inclusive.

Fig. 45

Fig. 46

Fig. 47

Fig. 48

Fig. 49

Fig. 50

Fig. 51

Pliers

Fig. 52

Fig. 53

3d Order

2d Order

1st Order

Fig. 54

Scraper
One of this no here drawn, and one only 8' long.

Fig. 55

J.K.Whildin del.

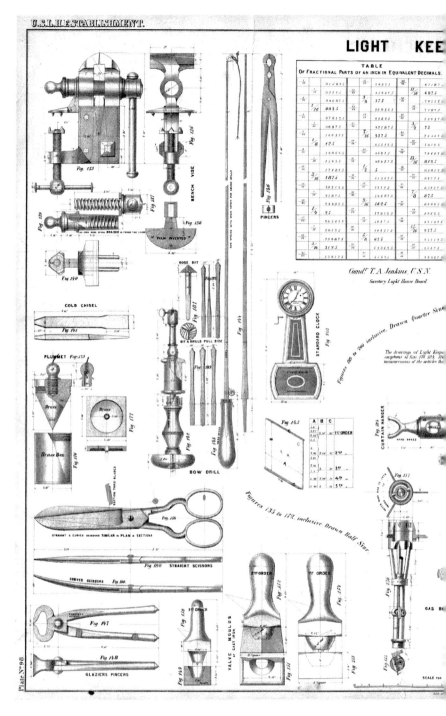

These United States Lighthouse Service drawings illustrate the myriad tools and devices utilized by light keepers. *Courtesy of the National Archives.*

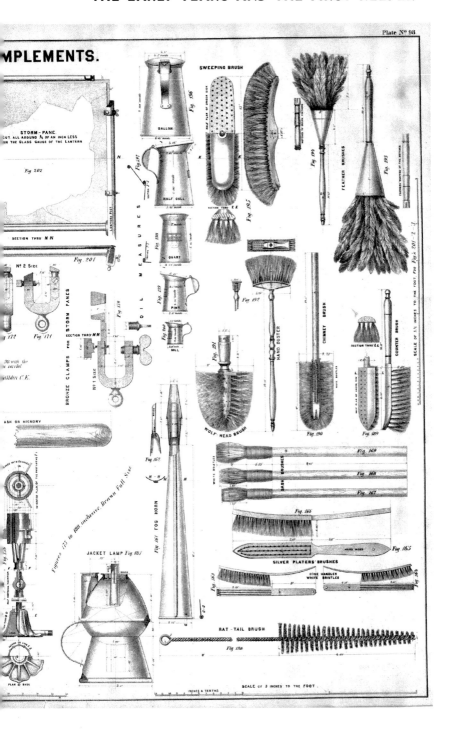

The gravestone of Benajah Wolcott at Wolcott Cemetery, several hundred yards northeast of Wolcott's stone house. The age and spelling are both incorrect. Benajah died at seventy. *Author's photo.*

family members to retrieve such bodies, which were dumped from ships. Wolcott frequently provided Christian burial for those bodies. His son William died of cholera at the same time.

His wife, Rachel, was subsequently named the first female light keeper on the Great Lakes. Her official appointment came on October 25, 1832. Rachel, familiar with her husband's work, kept the light for two seasons until resigning on February 14, 1834, the same day Jeremiah Van Benschoten was appointed keeper. Rachel Wolcott married Van Benschoten, a Vermilion widower, that year. The couple tended the light together until Van Benschoten resigned on August 4, 1841.

Roderick Williston followed, serving from August 4, 1841, until resigning September 19, 1843.

The list of chores required of keepers, which often included their families, was virtually endless. In addition to the nightly task during the shipping season of attending to the light, keepers were busy with the essential work of maintaining the property and general subsistence. Such jobs were often noted in the daily log and included a wide variety of repairs, maintenance and general domestic duties. Among the myriad tasks noted in keepers' logs over the years were cutting weeds, picking cherries and apples, mowing lawns, building a hitching post, whitewashing the tower, polishing various brass tools and fixtures, cleaning the tower ventilators, cleaning gutters and roofs, painting, wallpapering, building and repairing brick and stone structures, maintaining the cistern and the cellar, puttying windows, cutting wood, trimming shrubs, pulling vines, painting fences, stocking coal, cleaning the barn, burning brush, planting gardens, cleaning the stove, cleaning the boathouse, plowing gardens, cleaning the house and gathering dead fish. Trips to Sandusky and Port Clinton to obtain supplies were often noted.

In 1835, Pleasonton issued detailed instructions to light keepers nationwide. While it doesn't appear to have been an issue at Marblehead, keepers at some lighthouses failed to meet expectations. This "guide" spelled out keepers' duties in detail, leaving little room for imagination, speculation or deviation.

Instructions to the Keepers of Lighthhouses within the United States

1. You are to light the lamps every evening at sun-setting, and keep them continually burning, bright and clear, till sun-rising.

2. You are to be careful that the lamps, reflectors, and lanterns, are constantly kept clean, and in order; and particularly to be careful that no lamps, wood, or candles, be left burning anywhere as to endanger fire.

3. In order to maintain the greatest degree of light during the night, the wicks are to be trimmed every four hours, taking care that they are exactly even to the top.

4. You are to keep an exact amount of the quantity of oil received from time to time; the number of gallons, quarts, &c., consumed each night; and deliver a copy of the same to the Superintendent every three months, ending 31 March, 30 June, 30 September and 31 December, in each year with an account of the quantity on hand at the time.

5. You are not to sell, or permit to be sold, any spirituous liquors on the premises of the United States; but will treat with civility and attention, such strangers as may visit the Light-house [sic] under your charge, and as may conduct themselves in an orderly manner.

6. You will receive no tube-glass, wicks, or any other article which the contractors, Messr. Morgan & Co., at New Bedford, are bound to supply, which shall not be of suitable kind; and if the oil the supply, should, on trial, prove bad, you will immediately acquaint the Superintendent therewith, in order that he may exact from them a compliance with this contract.

7. Should the contractors omit to supply the quantity of oil, wicks, tube-glasses or other articles necessary to keep the lights in continual operation, you will give the Superintendent timely notice thereof, that he may inform the contractors and direct them to forward the requisite supplies.

8. You will not absent yourself from the Light-house at any time, without first obtaining the consent of the Superintendent, unless the occasion be so sudden and urgent as not to admit of an application to that officer; in that case, by leaving a suitable substitute, you may be absent for twenty-four hours.

9. All your communications intended for this office, must be transmitted through the Superintendent, through whom the proper answer will be returned.

Fifth Auditor and Acting Commissioner of the Revenue.

Treasury Department
Fifth Auditor's Office
April 23d, 1835

The same year, Secretary of the Treasury Levi Woodbury issued guidance to keepers of both sea and land lights on a variety of issues, including minimizing expenses; keeping stations clean, orderly and safe; and ensuring that no spirits are consumed on government properties. He also reminded keepers of their duties to render lifesaving assistance when able and to keep aware of the breach of United States revenue laws. In addition, Woodbury was keenly aware of the public relations component of lighthouse operations. He believed "civility should be enjoined as a duty to strangers wishing to examine the Lights."

From 1820 to 1852, Stephen Pleasonton directly controlled all lighthouses in the United States. While the fifth auditor was considered a frugal accountant who kept a close watch on taxpayer funds, many seriously questioned his expenditures on certain aspects of American lighthouses.

When Pleasonton first began managing the nation's maritime navigation system, there were 55 lighthouses and a handful of buoys. By 1852, there were 325 lighthouses, 35 lightships and hundreds of buoys. Most of these were on the Atlantic coast, and up until the last years of Pleasonton's tenure, they utilized Lewis's lamp systems.

Evidence suggests that Pleasonton at least inquired about the "new" Fresnel technology more than a decade before the first such lens arrived in the United States. As early as 1830, he had sent for information about Fresnel lenses. Subsequent correspondence gave Pleasonton the bad news; a First-order lens cost about $5,000, and a third-order lens cost about $2,000. Pleasonton's conservative economics would not allow him to spend such sums on the newer technology.

In a March 3, 1837 act, Congress questioned the need for some planned lighthouses that already had funds appropriated for construction. A board of naval commissioners was appointed to investigate the planned spending of $168,700 for navigation. At the next session of Congress, the board suggested that not all the lighthouses were needed and then recommended that thirty-one of the proposed lighthouse projects be postponed.

This led to President Martin Van Buren's creation of six Atlantic Coast districts and two Great Lakes districts, with each appointed a United States Revenue Cutter or a hired vessel and a naval officer to inspect and report the condition of all the lighthouses and navigation apparatus in each district.

The reports from the 1837 inquiry into the nation's lighthouses indicated that the administration and operation of lighthouses could be improved significantly. Lighthouse officials and elected leaders discussed the results of the reports for several years, though no significant actions came as a result of the inquiry. In a report to the Board of Navy Commissioners president dated August 18, 1837, Erie, Pennsylvania, Lieutenant G.J. Pendergrast wrote:

> *Sandusky Light-house* [sic].—*This is a highly important light, in consequence of its showing the entrance to Sandusky bay, and also as serving as a director through the island passage. There was a beacon-light authorized to have been placed as a guide into this harbor, and I have recommended, in my support on the subject, that it be made a red light, so as to distinguish it from Sandusky light-house, and have selected Cedar Point as the site for it. Four miles north of Sandusky light-house is Cunningham Island.*

In a July 7, 1838 act, Congress instructed Pleasonton to import two sets of lenticular apparatus and one set of reflector apparatus. The three systems had to be the best available. The two French lenses would be the first used in the United States. The plan was to conduct a careful experiment to see whether the costly Fresnel lenses would outperform, both in practicality and fuel costs, Winslow Lewis's light system. The two lenses were installed in lighthouses in Navesink, New Jersey, and cost almost $24,000—that included the services of a French technician who oversaw the installations, which were completed in March 1841. After evaluating the Fresnel lenses, Pleasonton offered a high opinion:

> *The cost of these lenses, however, is nothing compared to the beauty and excellence of the light they afford. They appear to be the perfection of apparatus for lighthouse purposes, having in view only the superiority of the light, which is reported by the pilots to be seen in clear weather a distance of forty miles.*

Naval officers continued to indicate the importance of the Sandusky Bay Light Station and its apparent good operation in their annual reports. On November 16, 1838, Lieutenant C.T. Platt wrote to the secretary of the treasury in Geneva, New York:

> *Sandusky Lighthouse has fifteen lamps, and thirteen lighted with thirteen bright reflectors, all in good order and fixed. The light is in commendable order, and the materials furnished by the contractor are faultless. This light-house* [sic] *is an important one, from its favorable location, in making the spacious bay of Sandusky.*

The South Passage became a critical lane for ships in the 1840s, as seen in *History of the Great Lakes*:

> *The glory of Sandusky harbor culminated during the 40's, when the city, then the northern terminus of the only north and south railway reaching the lakes…was also the terminus of the "floating palaces," plying between Buffalo and Sandusky and carrying all the travel to the southwest. The importance of this traffic is a tradition among the older navigators of the lakes.*

Stephen Woolverton, who had been awarded the contract to build the Sandusky Bay Light in 1821, went on to oversee the building of other lighthouses, including many on the Great Lakes. Apparently, he also dabbled in lamps. In December 1837 letters to Pleasonton, he indicated he was in possession of a great new product and that he had high hopes the United States Lighthouse Establishment would begin utilizing them. In a December 18 letter, Woolverton wrote:

> *My lamp is of a more simple, cheap and durable construction than those now in use (called Winslow Lewis Patent Lamp). The first cost of it will not exceed the one fourth part of that of W. Lewises, and the expense of keeping it in repair will not amount to one twentieth part than is does to keep the lamps now in use in repair.*

The letter closes with Woolverton's imploring Pleasonton not to enter into a contract to purchase any more Lewis lamps. By the end of the month, Woolverton penned a follow-up letter, enthusiastically selling his product and ideas:

Since writing you on the 18th last on the subject of my lamp for lighting up light houses, I have ascertained to my satisfaction that my lamp will consume at least six per cent less oil than Winslow Lewises [sic] Lamp does, the chandelier now in the lantern will do with a mere trifle of alteration in the fixture, to secure or set the lamp on, and a new chandelier will cost no more than those now in use. The wicks now on hand will answer, though in manufacturing them for my lamp, I would have them a little different.

Whatever new lamp system Woolverton developed or proposed to manufacture, apparently did not work out. Beyond minimal correspondence, little exists of his lamp or his plans for the lamp in records of the United States Lighthouse Establishment.

In 1845, the secretary of the treasury dispatched United States Navy Lieutenants Richard Bache and Thornton A. Jenkins to Europe to study lighthouse operations. They spent most of their time in England. When the pair returned, their recommendations included the appointments of an engineer and optician and district superintendents to assist the general superintendent in oversight of operations. The pair was also very interested in seeing Fresnel lenses replace the current Lewis lamps.

At the same time that Pleasonton's leadership of the nation's lighthouses was in the midst of years of congressional scrutiny, some of Woolverton's lighthouses had also come under fire for issues regarding engineering, construction and site placement. But his lighthouse on Sandusky Bay, more than two decades after it was constructed, was ably serving its purpose with no complaints raised against it.

The attractiveness of Lewis's system, despite its performance shortcomings, was its economy. Lewis had agreed to maintain the lights at half the cost of the previous system. The lamps consumed between thirty and forty gallons of oil annually. Thus, his lamp systems remained in place, despite their lackluster performance compared with the Fresnel lenses used in Europe.

Colonel Charles F. Drake kept the light burning from September 19, 1843, until he resigned on May 29, 1849. Historical accounts describe Colonel Drake as a "very eccentric gentleman of the old school, quite large, who stood very straight and had a very dignified and pompous manner of speech." Before becoming keeper at Marblehead, Drake owned and operated a tavern called Portland House at the Sign of the Golden Lamb in Sandusky.

Five years after Drake left the Marblehead Lighthouse, he kept the light at nearby Green Island Lighthouse. It was built in 1854 and began operating in

1855. On New Year's Eve 1863, Drake and his family had just begun dinner when they discovered the structure was on fire. They attempted to douse the flames with dozens of buckets of water, but their efforts were useless.

Drake and his family hastily gathered a few blankets, and at least one mattress, as the fire raged out of control. Temperatures were as low as twenty-five degrees below zero. That night, fifteen-foot-tall Lake Erie waves crashed against the shoreline; water froze in midair before falling to the ground. New Year's Eve revelers at the Doller Hotel on Put-in-Bay watched helplessly, including Pitt, Drake's son. Friends and partygoers restrained Pitt, who wanted to take a boat to Green Island immediately. In the morning, Pitt and others did make it to the island. There they found the Drake family alive, though suffering from frostbite and burns, camped in the outhouse. By July 1865, a new limestone structure was built, and the Drakes returned to Green Island to tend the new light for another six years.

When Drake left Marblehead in 1849, Captain Lodowick Brown, the son of an Irishman who had arrived in Philadelphia in 1805, succeeded him. Brown resigned on April 28, 1853. Little is known about Brown's time at the lighthouse. Personal correspondence indicates that one of Brown's grandchildren was born at the lighthouse on September 4, 1851.

By 1851, criticism of Pleasonton's Lighthouse Establishment had grown enough that a board was appointed to again examine American lighthouse operations. This led to the creation of the Lighthouse Board in October 1852. A 750-plus-page report examined keepers, supplies, locations, lighting apparatus, lightships and virtually every other facet of the United States Lighthouse Establishment (USLE). While the board praised Pleasonton's zealous penny-pinching, it found little else right with operations:

> *In investigating the subject confided to them, have endeavored to reach the truth from observation and research. That they have not done injustice to any one, they feel perfectly conscious; to have passed over palpable defects in the present management of our lights, involving great loss of human life and property, without pointing them out, would have been culpable and unpardonable; and that they have looked as leniently as possible on many points considered exceptionable, it is believed will be clearly shown by their report.*
>
> *The board have not sought so much to discover defects and point them out, as to show the necessity for a better system. Commerce and navigation, in which every citizen of this nation is interested, either directly or indirectly, claim it; the weather-beaten sailor asks it, and humanity demand it.*

Congress created the Lighthouse Board, assigning nine men who were disciplined in science, engineering or the military. Among the many changes, the newly formed board urged the use of Fresnel lenses. The previous year, Congress had authorized the secretary of the treasury to begin utilizing the lenses in new lighthouses if he deemed it appropriate.

While there were many lighthouse and USLE controversies during the nineteenth century, the tower and its keepers on Sandusky Bay in Marblehead remained largely untouched. While towers on the East Coast and Great Lakes crumbled from substandard construction or experienced serious settling issues due to poor placement, the tower at Marblehead remained steadfast. It was almost another half century before a major structural change visited the limestone tower.

The Lighthouse Board continued to keep close tabs on lighthouses and their keepers. Just two years after the creation of the board, minor changes were made at the Marblehead Lighthouse. For example, an 1854 inspector's report indicated that an improvement was made atop the tower: "Sandusky light-house [sic], copper ventilators were placed in the base of the lantern."

It was also just a few years before the lighthouse received the first of its two Fresnel lenses. The new lens was a direct result of the Lighthouse Board upgrading all lighting mechanisms in the nation's lighthouses. In 1858, the lighthouse was fitted with a barrel-shaped Fresnel lens just over twenty-eight inches tall. The fourth-order lens weighed between 441 and 661 pounds and had a radius just under ten inches. Worldwide, there were 889 such lenses manufactured. At the turn of the century, about 350 of the existing fourth-order lenses were located in United States lighthouses.

The new lens hosted a single lamp, fueled with lard oil. The days of Winslow Lewis's lamps were over. The new lamp and lens on the peninsula emitted a constant white light. This light was familiar to Great Lakes mariners for more than four decades, until the lighthouse received major upgrades around the turn of the century and became a flashing beacon instead of a constant beam.

An inspector's report from 1858 summed up the new Fresnel lens, "Important repairs have been made at Presque Isle, Grand River, Sandusky, and Grassy Island light-houses [sic], and other repairs of lesser importance have been made to various light-houses on Lake Ontario."

Jared B. Keyes was appointed keeper on April 28, 1853, and served until November 19, 1858. Keyes was born in Ontario County, New York, in 1815 and began a seafaring life as a young teenager aboard the schooner *Franklin*. By 1833, Keyes was master of the schooner *Thomas Morris*, and in 1837, he built a fifty-seven-ton ship, *Josephine*. In 1833, he married Arvilla Knapp Wolcott of Marblehead. She was the daughter-in-law of the first keeper, Benajah Wolcott, and his first wife, Elizabeth Bradley, and had previously been married to William Benajah Wolcott.

As most light keepers were, Keyes showed no fear when it came to helping others. On May 3, 1857, the 350-ton bark *Empire* was driven ashore near the lighthouse in a gale. The cargo of timber was lost when the vessel broke apart against the rocky shoreline. Keyes was highly commended for the effort he and a volunteer crew made to save the sailors who clung to the *Empire*'s masts as Lake Erie's wrath destroyed the ship and sent some of the sailors to their watery deaths.

The *Empire* was heading from Toledo to Tonawanda, New York, when it was caught in a gale north of the lighthouse. A *Sandusky Daily Commercial Register* account of the incident said the vessel was well east of Marblehead when the captain changed course in order to make it to the lee side of Kelleys Island, intending to take refuge from the storm. But in heavy seas and thick weather, the captain lost his bearings and, at 10:00 a.m., spied the breakers off Point Marblehead. Despite desperate maneuvers, the ill-fated ship eventually let go of both anchors and headed for land:

> As she was rapidly drifting roadside on shore, both anchors were let go, as soon as possible, and the vessel was brought head to wind, remaining in that position until 3 o'clock P.M., when, the sea is increasing, she commenced dragging—the waves making a clean breach over her at every surge. At ten minutes before four, she filled and capsized in deep water about one hundred and ten rods from Marblehead Light.
>
> The men took to the rigging where they clung as long as life lasted. Capt. Keyes lost no time in getting the life-boat [sic] into the water, which was manned with a stalwart crew. Just as the boat emerged from the first breakers, one of the oars broke, and Capt. K. replaced it with his steering oar; but before they got clear of white water, two other oars gave way, and they were obliged to put back to the shore, which they reached with great difficulty, the boat and men being landed "end over end" on the beach, by an enormous breaker.
>
> Meanwhile, the vessel had drifted further down shore, and as soon as fresh oars could be procured the life-boat was carried over land, and launched from another part of the beach. This time they succeeded in getting a line from the shore to the vessel, which had finally grounded. With great difficulty they got into the boat the only two who were left alive in the rigging,

and with them safely reached shore. One of the rescued—a seamen—was insensible when taken into the boat, but on reaching shore was restored. His name was Robert Moore. The other, Capt. Milligen, was in full possession of his faculties and strength, exhibiting wonderful powers of endurance. (Ten sailors and an orphan boy known only as Thomas were lost.)

W.L. Dayton served as keeper from February 1, 1859, until March 29, 1861, when he was removed. Details on why Dayton was removed are not known.

Thomas Dyer was appointed keeper on March 29, 1861. The Connecticut native brought his wife, Louisa, and two children to the lighthouse. During their tenure at the lighthouse, the Civil War came calling, and very close. The high-stakes, suspenseful drama was unknown to nearby residents and lasted just hours.

In general, Ohio was spared as the site of great battles and bloodshed during the war. But it was the site of a Union prison on Johnson's Island and a bold wartime plot. Just about two miles southwest of the lighthouse, standing in the shallow waters of Sandusky Bay, the four-hundred-acre island housed more than two thousand Confederate officers, far removed from the front lines for safekeeping. The closest action the lighthouse saw was the uneventful passing of a steamer en route to board a nearby Union warship in an effort to free thousands of prisoners.

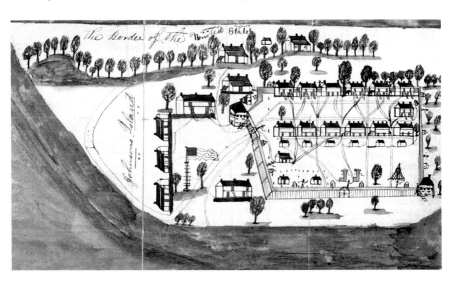

This watercolor by a Confederate prisoner illustrates the Union's Johnson's Island prison. *Courtesy of the Follett House Museum.*

On September 10, 1864, a Virginia native and former soldier who served under General "Stonewall" Jackson led a crew of pirates on a brazen mission deep inside Union territory. John Yates Beall and more than twenty men boarded the side-wheel steamer *Philo Parsons* as paying passengers at several different stops. After the ship made a stop at Kelleys Island, Beall and his crew commandeered the ship at gunpoint. They steamed toward Johnson's Island, almost twenty miles by water. The USS *Michigan*, a fourteen-gun warship usually anchored at the mouth of the bay, guarded the island. On that evening, it was anchored just where Beall had figured. As the *Philo Parsons* drifted toward the USS *Michigan* in darkness, with its engines shut down, its pirate crew waited for a signal from a conspirator aboard the warship.

But the signal, which was supposed to be a flare, never came. Beall's agent on the USS *Michigan* had been discovered, and he was likely already in the brig as the *Philo Parsons* drifted dangerously close to the warship. Beall and his crew, at the last moment, decided against launching the attack and, instead, fled back past the Marblehead Lighthouse toward the Detroit River and the relative safety of Canada.

Dyer died on December 12, 1865, and was replaced by Russell Douglas. Douglas's salary was set at $520. He kept the light for seven years, vacating the position on July 24, 1872. Lighthouse records indicate that Douglas was removed from the position due to advanced age. He was seventy-one or seventy-two at the time of his removal.

Thomas J. Keys replaced Douglas on August 27. It is not known who tended the light during the month when no keeper was appointed. Keys served until July 28, 1873, just a little under a year. Like Dyer, he was removed from the position, though the reason is not known.

An 1868 inspector's report listed several repairs and proposed improvements: "Sandusky.—Repair of plastering of keeper's dwelling has been authorized; a store-room for wicks, chimneys, paints and oils, is required. These articles are no longer kept in the kitchen." An inspector's report the next year indicated the station remained in good repair: "This station is in good condition. A boat-house will be built this season."

In the earliest years, the lighthouse had been called "Sandusky Lighthouse," "Sandusky Bay Lighthouse" and "Sandusky Bay Light Station." As early as 1849, nautical charts printed by the United States War Department's Bureau of Topographical Engineers referred to the lighthouse as "Marblehead." However, it wasn't until 1870 or 1871 that the official name was changed to "Marblehead Light Station" and "Marblehead Lighthouse."

Checking out the lake ice at the lighthouse has entertained men and women for almost two centuries. *Courtesy of the Sandusky Public Library and the Follett House Museum.*

Thomas J. Keys was appointed in August 1872 but did not stay long. While Keys tended the light, it was illuminated with four lamps, each with four-inch lenses. He kept the light for just under a year, leaving in July 1873. Keys was appointed at a salary of $500, $20 less than the previous keeper had been given six years earlier. More than two decades later, a column in a subsequent keeper's log that detailed previous keepers and their dates of appointment and departure listed both Keys and Douglas in a column titled "how vacated" as "removed."

The salary ranges for keepers varied greatly in the region. The Sandusky Range light keeper drew a salary of $580 in 1879, and between 1866 and 1872. But nearby Cedar Point light keepers earned salaries during those same years of either $400, $420, $520 or $560 annually. Nearby Vermilion and Huron keepers' salaries during the period also varied greatly, ranging from as low as $450 up to $560.

George H. McGee filled the position the same month Keys left and was one of the lighthouse's longtime stewards.

George and Johanna McGee came to the lighthouse in 1873. In September of that year, their first child was born in the stone keeper's house, which was now over fifty years old. Annual inspection reports indicated that the home had fallen into disrepair and that the McGees had constructed a "one-room shed in which the family is residing."

George McGee. *Courtesy of the Marblehead Lighthouse Historical Society.*

In 1880, the original keeper's house was razed and a new, two-story wood-frame structure was built. During the time George McGee spent as keeper, documents indicate he was quite a gardener. He planted potatoes, cabbage, tomatoes, peas, peppers, raspberries, currants, lettuce, potatoes and cherry trees, among other things. McGee is said to have built several boats during his time at the lighthouse, one of which he often rowed to the federal government's office in Sandusky. There, he turned in his time slips and any official lighthouse reports that were required.

The lighthouse logs kept by the McGees offer a wonderful glimpse into the lives of nineteenth-century light keepers. Following are excerpts from the McGees' lighthouse logs:

August 27, 1873. Heavy gale and big sea, NE cool and cloudy, very dark this evening. Painted the Comet and worked on the apparatus until 3:00 p.m. Large quantity of lumber commenced coming ashore at the station and on the beach for a while on either side. I saved several hundred feet, it is estimated that twenty-two thousand feet have come ashore on Marblehead.

September 8, 1873. Light changeable winds, cloudy, warm and moonlight tonight. I gave the top of the lantern a coat of red paint today. Carpenter worked all day on the barn.

September 9, 1873. Moderate easterly winds all day. Clear warm and moonlight tonight. I gave the outside of the lantern a coat of coal tar today, carpentry [sic] worked all day on the barn.

September 10, 1873. I gave the pedestal a coat of paint this a.m. I shingled ¾ of the day on the barn.

September 11, 1873. I whitewashed the barn today.

September 30, 1873. This day I do not work for Uncle Sam. The only important event which transpired today was the birth of a daughter weighing 8 pounds at 2:00 p.m.

December 31, 1873. I went to Sandusky today at 8:30 a.m. to mail reports and draw salary and returned at 8:00 p.m.

April 14, 1874. Cleaned the pedestal with emery paper, finished painting my boat which I have been building.

March 12, 1874. This afternoon a small boat with two men down the lake with ice. The wind was fresh NW and current running about 4 miles per hour. Freezing hard.

Around this time, the validity of a government deed had come into question regarding the right-of-way from the road traveling around the peninsula to the lighthouse property. In a May 1874 letter, United States attorney general George Henry Williams affirmed an August 1873 deed granting the right-of-way.

The lighthouse and the McGees were kept well supplied by *Haze*, the lighthouse tender that was assigned to the eleventh and twelfth districts. The government first purchased its own ships for tending lighthouses around 1840. The 137-foot *Haze* was commissioned on October 16, 1867. With a beam of 24 feet, 7 inches; a draft of 8 feet, 4 inches; and a displacement of 328 tons, it is difficult to believe the vessel was powered solely with a 292 brake horse power, single-propeller, coal-fired boiler. The purchase price of the *Haze*, originally traveling as the private vessel *Merchant*, was $27,000.

The Lighthouse Board resupplied lighthouses on a quarterly basis. In the beginning, lighthouses were resupplied by private vessels contracted for the service. They delivered lighthouse supplies, including wicks and fuel—which, at the time, was whale oil produced by the American whaling fleet in the Atlantic Ocean. Each lighthouse keeper was afforded an annual allotment of staples that included two barrels of flour, fifty pounds of rice, fifty pounds of brown sugar, twenty-four pounds of coffee, two hundred pounds of pork, one hundred pounds of beef, ten gallons of peas or beans, four gallons of vinegar and two barrels of potatoes and salt. The food and the official light supplies were delivered together.

The *Haze* was decommissioned on March 15, 1905, and sold the next year. Its crew immediately boarded the *Crocus*, a longer, wide, faster, deeper, steel-hulled vessel with two steam engines. The *Crocus* served lighthouses and navigational aids in the tenth district for the next four decades. Lighthouse tenders were typically named after flowers, trees and shrubs.

As the years passed, the McGees kept the lighthouse well tended and left plenty of interesting entries in their logs to entertain and inform those who might be interested:

June 25, 1874. Off in the country hunting my cow.

April 29, 1875. Steamer Haze *came to Clemmons dock at 5:30 a.m. Loaded stone barge, anchored and cleaned up at 1:00 p.m. Fearful gale NW. A scow dismasted her foremast about two miles E of this station. The water has been very low today breaking up shell rock at the foot of the boat storage.*

May 1, 1875. A vessel sunk about 1-½ miles north of the station at 11:30 a.m. Gales NE a.m., S to W p.m., NW tonight. Rainy, 5 lives lost (schooner Consuelo *from Cleveland to Toledo with sandstone. Two men rescued by LS crew.)*

June 19, 1875. Steamer Gazelle *layed cable from Marblehead to Kelley's* [sic] *Island this p.m.*

July 8, 1875. Steamer Haze *stopped at this station at 7:50 p.m. and cleared at 8:30 p.m. Com. Doller, Capt. Davis (of the Lighthouse Board), J. McCarran inspected the station.*

July 15, 1875. Went to Sandusky to take wife and children. Went in rowboat 10:00 a.m., returned at 5:00 p.m.

August 10, 1875. Went to camp ground [sic] *meeting at Put-in-Bay.*

August 17, 1875. Went to Sandusky to see Pound Boat regatta.

August 25, 1875. Schooner Mayflower *sunk about 1 mile S of the W end of Kelley's Island. Loaded with stone.*

September 5, 1875. Cleaned apparatus and fountains and burners.

September 6, 1875. Helped Sam Wilson thrash wheat and oats.

September 7, 1875. Helped Phillip Smith thrash wheat and oats.

September 12, 1875. Cleaned lantern glass and tower.

September 23, 1875. Went to Erie County fair 3:00 a.m. to 5:00 p.m.

October 30, 1875. Steamer Germania *landed 6 tons of coal on the beach.*

January 7, 1876. Extinguished the light this morning according to regulations.

January 12, 1876. The passage is full of ice.

Chapter 4

HEROIC ACTS AND A NEW
LIFE-SAVING STATION

In J.B. Mansfield's *History of the Great Lakes*, published in 1899, the Western Basin was described as an especially dangerous place for mariners: "The most dangerous place in Lake Erie is in the neighborhood of Point Pelee, near the western extremity of the lake. Off the point lies, like a satellite, Point Pelee Island; between the two is a shoal. Point, shoal and island cause many wrecks each year."

Historical accounts prove this true, with serious groundings and sinkings recorded by the hundreds. In just nine years, from 1867 to 1876, at least nineteen such serious maritime disasters were recorded in the area, including two at North Bass Island, three at Middle Bass Island, six at Kelleys Island, five at Cedar Point, one at Put-in-Bay and two at Marblehead.

Most such incidents on the lake involved loss of life, such as the capsizing of *Monarch of the Glen*, a forty-two-foot schooner that sank off the Marblehead Peninsula in a November 1862 gale. The entire crew of five perished in the icy waters. During the nineteenth century, the lake was rife with ships and their captains and crews foiled by fires, explosions, hard and soft groundings, hull failures, collisions and all manner of chaos and destruction at the hands of waves, wind, snow, rain and ice.

In 1875, a great loss of life occurred during a spring storm. The May 6, 1875 *Detroit Free Press* gave an account of the *Consuelo*'s sinking:

> *From Capt. Danger, of the tug* Winslow, *which is at work at Kelley's* [sic] *Island trying to raise the schr.* Exchange *at that port, the following*

particulars are received of the sinking of the schr. Consuelo *last Saturday morning. A living gale of wind from the southwest was sweeping over the lake that morning and the* Consuelo *was sighted making the harbor at Sandusky, being at that time about three miles from Marblehead Light, in the South passage. She seemed to be making good headway until suddenly she listed and for some time went wild, those aboard of her being unable, apparently, to handle her. At times she would show her keel, causing those on land to conclude that she had shifted her cargo. As soon as this conclusion was reached Capt. Danger decided to go to her relief, owing to the gale the* Winslow *was lying at the dock idle and was obliged to get up her steam. This requires some time, and it was while the* Winslow *was getting up steam that the* Consuelo *filled and went down, righting as she sunk and striking on an even keel. In about 10 minutes after she sunk, the* Winslow *was under way and reached the scene in a short time, meeting the Clemons brothers, of Marblehead, who had put out from shore in a small boat, and rescued Frederick Donahue and James Kin. After cruising about for some time without discovering any of the bodies, the* Winslow *proceeded to the wreck and took off a tin box containing the captain's papers, another box containing the cook's jewelry, and three trunks beside a small bureau. The* Winslow *was then met by the stmr.* Hickox, *bound from Cleveland, who took Donahue and King aboard and then went to the sunken schooner and took away a portion of their upper works. The names of the persons drowned are H.M. Hauser, Captain; Wm. Clary, Wm. Low and Chas. Peterson, seamen; and the woman cook, name unknown. The captain leaves a wife and daughter at Milwaukee, and the cook's home was in Buffalo. The* Consuelo *was an old schooner of 195 tons burthen, built at Cleveland in 1851 by R. Calkins for O'Neil & Co., and was calculated at that time at $3,500. In 1861 she underwent large repairs, being almost entirely rebuilt. She was considered a seaworthy craft, the only thing against her being her age.*

While the *Winslow* and *Hickox* did what they could, it was three brothers—Lucien, Ai and Hubbard Clemons—who had acted heroically, setting out from shore in gale conditions in a small, shallow rowboat, risking their lives against great odds. One account tells that Lucien Clemons saw the *Consuelo* capsize from an attic window as he worked on a gunstock during the violent storm, which had forced him inside. The *U.S. Lifesaving Service's Annual Report for the Year Ending June 30, 1876* offers the official account of the daring feat:

The medals of the first class were bestowed upon Messrs. Lucien M. Clemons, Hubbard M. Clemons, and Ai J. Clemons, of Marblehead, Ohio, three brothers, who displayed the most single gallantry in saving two men from the wreck of the schooner Consuelo, *about two miles north of that place, on May 1, 1875. The schooner* Consuelo *was a staunch craft of 450-tons burden, which had made a voyage across the Atlantic to Liverpool in the early 1860s, and had out-ridden fierce tempests on that stormy ocean many times. On this day, however, she was caught in a fierce gale about twelve miles from Sandusky, and three miles*

This portrait, likely taken at the turn of the century, shows Lucien Clemons with his Gold Life-Saving Medal. *Courtesy of Boyd Weber.*

north of the rock shores of Marblehead. Between Kelley's island [sic] *and Marblehead the water is nowhere deeper than thirty feet, and consequently, in nautical parlance, "a nasty sea" comes up very quickly in a gale.*

It appears from the evidence of the transaction that the schooner, which was heavily laden with blocks of stone, was seen by a number of spectators on the shore laboring in apparent distress in the passage between Kelley's Island [sic] *and Marblehead, the sea at the time being tremendous and the wind blowing a gale from the northeast.* [The *Consuelo*'s cargo had been hastily and improperly stowed, and either through carelessness or to facilitate unloading, rollers had been left under some of the massive blocks of stone in the hold. The vessel pitched and tossed so violently that these blocks and the whole cargo shifted, and suddenly, almost without warning, the boat gave a lurch and foundered.]

The captain, three men and the cook were at once lost, but Mate Donahue and one of the sailors succeeded in clinging to the spars, where they were sighted from Marblehead by Captain Clemons and his brothers. These remaining two soon succeeded in getting a hold in the cross-trees of the mainmast, which were above water, where they clung for nearly an hour hoping for rescue. It was then that the three heroic brothers took a small flat-bottomed skiff, twelve feet long, three feet wide, and fifteen inches deep, the only boat available on the coast, and leaving their weeping wives and children, who formed a part of the watching group of forty or fifty persons on the shore, went out in this frail shell to the rescue. Family members and onlookers watched in fear as the shallow craft disappeared time and again in the rollers, only to reemerge once again. It seemed as if their frail craft must certainly swamp, but they kept steadily on until they were about exhausted.

The venture was, in the judgment of the lookers on, several of them old sailors themselves, hazardous in the extreme, but after nearly an hour's hard struggle with the waves, the Clemons brothers gained the wreck and delivered the two exhausted men from their perilous position in the rigging. However, the danger was by no means past, as the strength of the two men was entirely spent, and the storm was increasing in its merciless fury.

With the added weight in their skiff they were then unable to make the shore. They remained for a long time tossing about upon the high sea in momentary danger of destruction, when fortunately they were spotted by the steam-tug Winslow *which came to their assistance and landed them safely at Kelley's Island* [sic].

The Clemons brothers lived on 133 acres in Marblehead with their parents, Alexander and Almariah, who had moved from the Sandusky area in 1834. Alexander Clemons, like Wolcott, purchased land that had once been owned by Epahroditus Bull. Alexander Clemons and his brothers were the first to quarry stone on Kelleys Island and later began quarrying stone on another parcel of land in what is now Danbury Township. By 1850, his business enterprises had grown considerably, and Clemons took his sons Hubbard, Lucien, Ai and Albert into the quarry business. United States Post Office Department records indicate Alexander Clemons was appointed postmaster in Marblehead that same year.

Clemons was a man of faith and is considered one of the earliest founders of the nearby Methodist community, Lakeside. The community was officially established several years after he died. Clemons's campfire prayer meetings are still popular today. His deep belief in Christian principles is likely the source of the hard work ethic and selfless attitudes of his sons. On June 20, 1874, Congress created medals to honor people who endangered themselves at sea in order to rescue others. The awards were designated in two classes, one for "cases of extreme and heroic daring" and the other for "cases not so distinguished." They were gold and silver medals, respectively.

Lucien Clemons's original Gold Life-Saving Medal. *Courtesy of Boyd Weber.*

After the *Consuelo* incident, the Clemons brothers were subsequently awarded the first three Gold Medals for Life-Saving on June 19, 1876. Each medal, designed by German-born United States Mint engraver Anthony C. Paquet, was four and one-quarter inches in diameter. One side features three men rescuing a sailor and a wrecked ship. The other side of Lucien's features a monument inscribed with his name and the date of the *Consuelo*'s sinking. It is assumed the medals of Ai and Hubbard are each inscribed with their names.

At the same time, two others also received the medal, though they were awarded the silver, or second-class lifesaving medal. Those men had rowed offshore at Watt's Ledge in Maine in a sixteen-below-zero gale, pulled two men from an offshore ledge and delivered them, barely alive, to safety, having rowed more than two miles.

Until lifesaving stations or other such systems were established, it was expected that lighthouse keepers would render assistance to a vessel in distress. That is, they would identify the need and subsequently organize a rescue party and oversee rescue operations.

The first American lifeboat was a thirty-foot-long whaleboat, rowed by ten men and guided with steering oars, stationed at the nation's first lifeboat station in Cohasset, Massachusetts. The Massachusetts Humane Society operated the station. While the society's efforts saved many lives in Massachusetts, it did not help mariners elsewhere. In 1848, Congress approved $10,000 for "surfboats, rockets, carronades [line-throwing mortars], and other necessary apparatus for the better preservation of life and property from shipwrecks on the coast of New Jersey." Between 1849 and 1855, more stations were established along the nation's East Coast, with most in New York and New Jersey. The volunteer-staffed sites often fell into disrepair, were utilized for personal use and were generally disorganized. Because the system relied on volunteers, drills and practice were scarce, and rescuers were not always present when needed.

During the brutal winter of 1870–71, a number of high-profile shipwrecks occurred, prompting Congress to appropriate $200,000 to help establish a paid lifesaving system that spring. The move authorized the secretary of the treasury to employ paid crews and build lifesaving stations wherever he deemed necessary. Later that year, Sumner Kimball was appointed head of the Revenue Marine Bureau, which would later become the United States Coast Guard. He was in charge of both lifesaving stations and revenue cutters.

Marblehead, the site of numerous shipwrecks over the years, would soon be home to an official government-operated lifesaving station staffed with full-time professionals. On June 24, 1876, property for the station was purchased from John H. James Jr. Klam Schwartz and Co. constructed the station, following a nationwide standard design. The construction was described, in part, in *Popular Science Monthly*, volume 182, no. 15, "Built of tongued and grooved pine, with gable roofs, covered with cypress or cedar shingles, and strong shutters to the windows, and are securely bolted to a foundation of cedar or locust posts, sunk in trenches four feet deep."

The station was fully equipped for lifesaving missions and included anchors, grapnels, axes, boathooks, cots, preservers, pikes, wrecking tools and plenty of lines of various types. The first floor included a large room, housing the surfboat, with double doors opening onto a ramp facing the lake. There were two smaller first-floor rooms as well, one for the keeper and the other for an eight-man crew. The second floor contained sleeping quarters and storage space for smaller equipment items. The total cost for the Marblehead station was about $4,500.

On September 9, 1876, the new lifesaving station was officially opened. The Point Marblehead Life-Saving Station was located about one mile west of the lighthouse and about one-third of a mile east of the current site of the United States Coast Guard's Station Marblehead.

Lucien Clemons, who had led his brothers on the daring *Consuelo* rescue, was an obvious choice for the leadership position and was appointed commander of the new lifesaving station at a rate of $200 annually. A United States Treasury letter dated July 2, 1878, reappointed Clemons as keeper of the lifesaving station at a rate of $400 annually. A United States Treasury letter dated September 5, 1882, again reappointed Lucien Clemons as keeper of Life-saving Station Nine at a significant salary increase, with an annual salary of $600.

Indeed, the Clemons brothers had acted heroically in their rescue of the *Consuelo*'s survivors. But the incident in Marblehead was neither the first nor last time the *Consuelo* met trouble on the seas. As was common in the nineteenth century, ships met with disasters frequently, and only the worst of the worst meant the end of the line for a wooden ship. From hard and soft groundings to fires, collisions and sinkings, the seas took their tolls.

In 1854, the *Consuelo* damaged a bowsprit in a collision with the schooner *A. Ford*. Fifteen years later, it sunk on the Maumee River in Toledo after a collision with a bridge abutment. Five years later, the *Consuelo* sunk again near Kelleys Island. That is where the Clemonses met it on rough seas to save two lives and earn their lifesaving medals. Five years later, in 1885, it sunk at North Channel on Lake Huron. Two years after that, it was driven ashore at Bailey's Harbor, Wisconsin, and later that year, it ground ashore at Suelchoix Point, again on Lake Huron. In November 1887, *Consuelo* finally met its match when it was driven ashore near the harbor at Port Hope, Michigan, on Lake Huron. The crew abandoned the ship in a gale, and it broke apart on shore over several days. There was no raising or rebuilding of the *Consuelo* after the Port Hope gale.

Public sentiment in favor of the establishment of a lifesaving service had been growing and, by 1878, had reached a crescendo after the public became weary of shipwrecks in which mariners were often left to their own

This 1879 etching by M.J. Burns illustrates the treacherous work awaiting crew members at lifesaving stations. *Courtesy of the National Archives.*

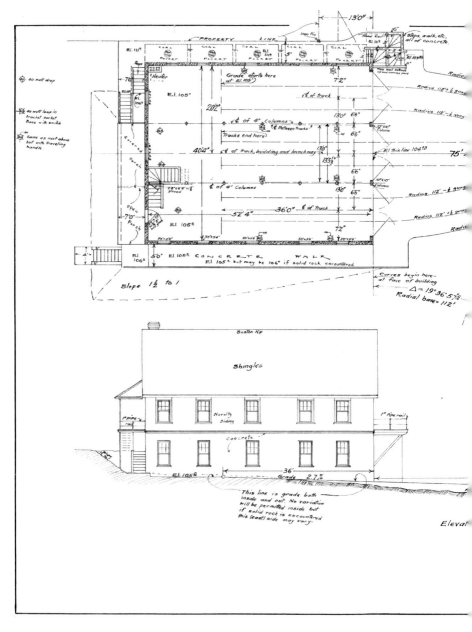

An architectural drawing illustrates the USCG's plans for a new boathouse, circa 1915.
Courtesy of the National Archives.

devices. In addition, the financial losses of shipwrecks had been rising for years. In 1857, $1.38 million was lost in 481 incidents on the Great Lakes.

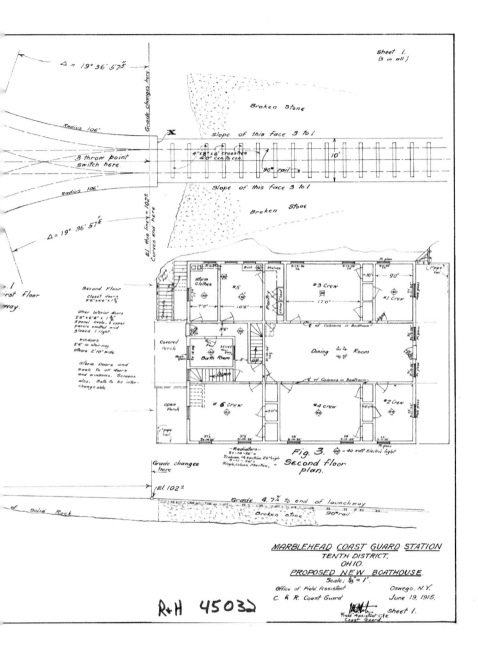

Fig. 3.
Second floor plan.

MARBLEHEAD COAST GUARD STATION
TENTH DISTRICT,
OHIO.
PROPOSED NEW BOATHOUSE.
Scale; ⅛ = 1'.
Office of Field Assistant   Oswego, N.Y.
C. & R. Coast Guard   June 19, 1915.
                                        sheet 1.
Field Assistant C&R.
Coast Guard

R+H 45032

Prior to 1878, a patchwork of systems had been established along the United States coastlines for assisting mariners. Some areas had established houses of refuge where shipwrecked seamen who were able to make it ashore could find food, shelter and water. Other areas established lifeboat stations, usually located only near busy ports. The small stations included items that could be used in case of shipwreck, including small boats. In an emergency, volunteers from the area could gather and utilize the stations' property to aid in rescues.

On June 18, 1878, Congress unanimously passed the Act to Organize the Life-Saving Service. The new service—a formal, national system—was placed under the Treasury Department and drew together the many facets of localized lifesaving services that had developed during the previous decades, including the Point Marblehead Life-Saving Station. When compared to the volunteer-based systems, the United States Life-Saving Service's (USLS) worth was obvious: there was an 87.5 percent decrease in shipwreck deaths within the areas covered by the service.

During its forty-four years of service before becoming part of the United States Coast Guard (USCG) in 1915, the USLS is credited with aiding more than 178,000 people in peril. And at Point Marblehead Life-Saving Station, Clemons certainly kept his station in good order and ready to serve.

In general, his daily logbook was detailed. Each day, Clemons kept track of all the vessels passing by the lifesaving station and the number of vessels entering and departing Sandusky's port. In the total count of passing ships, he noted the numbers by type: barges, barks, sloops, schooners and steamers. But in the ships entering and leaving the nearby port, he noted them in just two groups: steamers and schooners. For each day during the shipping season, the wind, weather and sea conditions were noted four times: at midnight, sunrise, noon and sunset.

Many of the entries in the logbooks kept at the lifesaving station were rather boring and consisted of notations on uneventful weather, vessels sighted and chores completed around the site. Regularly noted tasks included drying and readying ropes and routine maintenance of the surfboats, as well as painting and other maintenance jobs. Clemons noted all training in his log, such as the following three entries:

Monday October 27th, 1879
This day the crew of No. 9 had their regular drill all of the crew being present & drilled them in the use of the Life Boat & in the mortar drill one shot was fired with the Lyle gun with 2 oz. of powder which threw the line over the practice spar. The ball going the distance of 223 yards.

Friday October 31ˢᵗ, 1879
This day the Keeper & Surfman No 1 was engaged in getting everything in order at the station & drying the sails of the Life Boat. Received by mail one copy of the New Regulations.

Saturday November 1ˢᵗ, 1879
This day the Keeper & Surfman No 1 was engaged in looking over the Rules & Regulations in regard to the resuscitation of the apparently drowned.

Of course, a good many of the station's entries offered more excitement than a few lines about daily maintenance chores, training and reading up on rules and regulations:

Thursday October 3ʳᵈ, 1879
This day the crew was called to go to the assistance of a Canadian Scow which was discovered capsized about three miles N & E of the Station. All of the crew was on hand and ready in 10 minutes after the signal was given. The crew of the Scow was taken off by the Steamer Barge Bay City *about ten minutes before we got to the wreck. We went to the Barge to see if we could do anything for them and the Capt. of the Barge thought we had better take the crew of the Scow to Sandusky as one of them was badly hurt and nearly deceased. After giving him some brandy and getting him ready we took all of the crew in the life boat and went to the city where the capt of the Scow could get a tug to go and tow the wreck to some place of safety then we returned to the station.*

Thursday November 20ᵗʰ, 1879
The crew of Life Boat Station was called out between eleven & 12 o'clock to assist the crew of the Scow C. Rich *after they were cared for the Schooner* New Hampshire *was discovered dragging ashore so we hastened to help them all we could and arrived just in time to save the Capt. who undertook to come ashore in the Schooner's small boat and was unable to get out and had to be taken out by our crew of the Life Boat Station after this crew was cared for the Scow* JH Saunders *of Port Huron was discovered ashore we went to them but they did not want to get off as the Scow was all right and not pounding so then we went to the Station and kept a good lookout until day light. The lights used at the station was of no account so could not keep them burning.*

Despite the fact that most logbook entries were uneventful, and a few were very exciting, some were surprisingly honest:

Saturday December 6th, 1879
This day there was nothing done at the Station but to count the names in the visitors Register.

Saturday December 13th, 1879
This day there was nothing done at the station.

An October, 15, 1884 *Norwalk Daily Reflector* article chronicled more heroic efforts on the lake:

The life-saving crew at Point Marblehead is as able and courageous as there is on the lake. They did excellent service during the storm. They saved the life of the captain of the scow Keyes, *who was swept overboard just before his vessel went on the beach, after which they alone rescued the three men whose pound boat capsized two miles off shore; after they had got the men in the life boat and were making for the shore, the tug* Mystic *came up and took the rescued party into port. The crew is as good a one as there is on the lake.*

In addition to Clemons and his crews saving lives, they regularly saved businesses tens of thousands of dollars. On October 12, 1895, the schooner *E.C. Roberts* grounded on Starve Island Reef in a gale. After being towed eight and a half miles out by the tug *John E. Monk*, the lifesaving crew was able to remove the four-man *Roberts* crew and get them to Kelleys Island. After the gale broke, the lifesaving crew was able to free the schooner from the reef, saving both the vessel and its cargo, valued at $7,500. Just a $1,000 loss was incurred in the incident. Sometimes, the crew performed the grim work of recovering the bodies of drowning victims, as they did in July 1898, recovering the bodies of two young campers whose rowboat capsized in the channel.

Clemons and his crew members are credited with seventy major missions on Lake Erie during his tenure. Those daring missions include a September 1883 meeting with the *William St. John*, a thirty-one-ton steamer en route from Leamington to Sandusky with a cargo of fish. After missing the channel, it ran aground at Sandusky Bay near the Cedar Point Light. The crew rowed five miles to the scene, finding another steamer nearby. The crew members were unable to get a line to the *William St. John*. They rowed back to the station for a longer line and, after returning to the wreck, worked for four hours to get the vessel off the sandbar.

Not all of Clemons's rescues involved vessels. More than a century before a 2009 large-scale rescue of ice fishermen on the Western Basin received worldwide media coverage, Clemons and a volunteer crew saved lives on the ice. The shipping season and the lifesaving station were both closed, but the volunteers headed onto the lake to search for four men. Accounts say they pushed a surfboat across the ice some distance to get it into the water and then rowed to the site where the Kelleys Island residents were drifting on an ice floe. A letter signed by Henry Elfres, J. Hemmeline, H.F. Schnell and Frank C. Reinhart read, "This is to certify that the Point Marblehead life-saving crew on February 20, 1888, came to our rescue when we had given up all hopes and expected to be carried down the lake in the ice and lost."

In all, Clemons and his professional lifesaving crew members are credited with saving at least eighty-nine lives on Lake Erie waters during his twenty years of service at the lifesaving station. They also saved about $400,000 (more than $10 million if adjusted for inflation) in cargoes and vessels. In an *Inland Seas* article titled "Heroism at Marblehead," Merlin Wolcott described his uncle:

> *Lucien was a man of quiet dignity in his brass-buttoned navy blue uniform with a shining lifesaving insignia on his duck-billed cap. He liked the warmth of a sailor's turtle-necked knitted sweater which he frequently wore with the uniform vest and coat. His most distinguished feature was his goatee. All his long life he wore chin whiskers which lightened with the years. Although I was very young when I first met him, I remember his quiet reserve. He was no idle chatterer, although he especially enjoyed talking about the Lakes and sailing.*

Interestingly, Winslow W. Griessler, one of Clemons's surfmen, went on to do great things. An 1893 letter from the lifesaving district superintendent asked Lucien Clemons his opinion on whether Griessler was a good man to command the new Niagara Life-Saving Station, which was nearing completion at the time. Just a few years later, in 1900, Griessler earned his own gold lifesaving medal for his own remarkable feat on Lake Erie at the Buffalo Life-Saving Station.

Clemons was well respected, and his opinion was often solicited, such as an 1894 inquiry from the USLS superintendent. The letter asked Clemons to assess a new twenty-six-foot self-righting boat, and to report his findings as soon as possible.

Clemons retired in 1897 after more than two decades of service. After the death of Captain David Dobbins, superintendent of the Ninth Life-Saving District, Clemons was recommended for the position by former president Rutherford B. Hayes. Hayes wrote "the qualifications, experience and record of L.M. Clemons justifies recommendation." Clemons did not receive the appointment but appeared content with his position in command of the Point Marblehead Life-Saving Station during the remainder of his service.

In 1921, a large, modern limestone station was constructed about half a mile west of the original Point Marblehead station. In 1982, an even larger and more modern station was constructed at that site and is currently in service. The station consistently ranks as one of the busiest USCG sites in the nation, regularly assisting hundreds of vessels each year.

As the Point Marblehead Life-saving Station came into existence, the nearby lighthouse remained, and the McGees continued to document their daily lives:

February 26, 1876. Went to Wilson's dance last night.

March 10, 1876. Steamer Golden Eye *commenced running between the islands and Sandusky.*

March 23, 1876. Supt. of Construction of Life Boat Houses here this P.M.

April 1, 1876. Captain John McCarran visited the station to inspect the site for a proposed Life Boat Station.

May 12, 1876. Whitewashed dining room, chicken coop and coal shed.

May 2, 1877, Planted ½ bunch each of potatoes, cabbage, tomato, pepper, peas and lettuce seed.

May 4, 1877. Set 10 raspberry roots (Clark's Red and Clack Caps) also 10 currant bushes.

May 11, 1877. Lake Survey Boat Ada *came to anchor at sunrise and landed 25 officers and men to work on this coast. They all camped at Ward's Point.*

June 3, 1877. Steamer Ada *moved survey camp from Marblehead to Kelley's [sic] Island this a.m.*

August 30, 1878. Hotel burned at Put-in-Bay tonight.

Chapter 5

A NEW KEEPER'S HOUSE

After the lighthouse was built, commerce and travel on Lake Erie increased. The cities and villages in the area grew as more Americans headed west and populations rose. All the while, keepers and their families moved into, and out of, the keeper's house, which sat in the shadow of the lighthouse. Over time, the condition of the home deteriorated significantly. An 1877 inspector's report indicated that the keeper's house was in dire need of either repair or rebuilding:

> *1877. Marblehead, Sandusky Bay, Lake Erie, Ohio.—This station is in bad condition. The house is old, leaky and barely habitable. It should be rebuilt. This is one of the most important lights on Lake Erie, all vessels passing through the lake to the southward of the islands must make it, and it must always be kept up. The tower is also in bad condition. The estimated cost of rebuilding the station is $20,000, and an appropriation of that amount is recommended.*

For several years, inspectors continued to note the poor condition of the home. An inspection the following year documented:

> *1878. Marblehead, Sandusky Bay, Lake Erie, Ohio. The dwelling and outer wall of the tower are in bad condition. The house is not habitable in cold weather and is unfit for use as a dwelling at any time. A small frame shed of one room was put up last year, and this the keeper and his family*

This photograph, which appears to have been taken from the water, shows the new keeper's house. It was taken before the new lantern was installed. *Courtesy of Phillip Teitlebaum.*

occupy during cold weather. The new dwelling and tower recommended by the board in its last annual report are urgently needed. This is one of the most important stations on the lakes, as the channel between it and the islands is the thoroughfare for all vessels passing up and down the lake, except those running directly between Eastern ports and the Detroit River. An appropriation of $20,000 is required to put the station in proper order.

The following year, an inspection again found the keeper's house severely wanting. A Lighthouse Service ledger indicates that repairs were made at Marblehead, though it does not enter into great detail. The records show that, in November 1879, repairs were made to outbuildings and fences, and a chimney cap was replaced on the home. The next spring, boat ways were repaired, and an old stone fence on the property was removed. In June, the icehouse was repaired and painted, and boat ways were repaired again, this time including a paint job. A new floor was installed in the boathouse, and a smoke conductor was converted into a ladder. The McGees continued to record the lighthouse's history:

April 30, 1879. A three-masted schooner capsized in the passage between this station and Kelley's [sic] Island at 3:00 a.m. loaded with hickory butts. Crew taken off by yawl boat from passing barge and taken to Sandusky by Life Boat No. 9. Gale NW. Tug Mystic *is towing the wreck into Sandusky tonight.*

September 2, 1879. Heavy gale with snow set in last night at 10:00 o'clock. Gale NE today. Three vessels ashore last night between this station and the Life Boat Station. Tender Haze *came up the lake. I went to Sandusky at noon.*

December 2, 1879. Tugs Myrtle *and* Mystic *pulled schooner* New Hampshire *off the beach this p.m. and towed her to Sandusky. She was one of the vessels which came ashore on the 20th of last month.*

February 10, 1880. Cedar Point relit tonight. Green Island has been lit for several nights.

May 5, 1880. The lights in this station went out between 2 o'clock this morning and sunrise. Trimmed at 11 last night. Looked at light from the dwelling at 2:00. Cannot account for the accident. Dead calm last night.

May 24, 1880. U.S. Tender Haze *delivered supplies to this station this p.m. The lard oil lamps were taken down and mineral oil lamps substituted. Commander Bridgeman and Capt. D.P. Heap inspected the station.*

The steamship *R.B. Hayes* passes near the Marblehead Lighthouse en route to Cedar point in 1905. *Courtesy of the Ottawa County Historical Museum.*

By September 1880, "foundation of new dwelling commenced," and in October, "work on keeper's new dwelling continued." Work on the new home continued through November and was completed in December. A locker room was furnished somewhere in the light tower, and all that remained, the ledger indicates, was "two or three days painting." The ledger also indicates that a leak in the tower was addressed and that boat ways were once again repaired.

By January, painting and varnishing at the new keeper's residence had been completed. Throughout 1881, other improvements were made to the new dwelling, including painting outside and the kitchen floor and varnishing of stairs. Wire screens were later installed on doors and windows of both the dwelling and the tower. During this construction period, the old keeper's home remained intact but was razed in June 1882. The same month, ninety feet of boardwalk leading from the dwelling to the tower and the boathouse was laid.

The Lighthouse Service issued updated employee instructions in 1881 and was apparently aware of the increasing number of visitors at lighthouses around the nation. The instructions implored keepers and assistants to treat visitors with courtesy and politeness and warned against other things, such as allowing visitors to handle the apparatus or carve their names on the lantern glass or tower windows. Additionally, intoxicated persons were to be removed "by the employment of all proper and reasonable means."

September 20, 1880. C.W. Channing and laborers arrived p.m. and commenced excavating cellar for new dwelling.

October 5, 1880. Scow **H.A.** Sammars *went ashore and sunk ½ mile NW of Lt. House p.m. in trying to get away from the dock.*

October 8, 1880. Steam pump raised the Sammars *today, Tug towed her off and placed her alongside the dock.*

October 9, 1880. Sammars *sunk alongside the dock last night.*

July 2, 1881. President Garfield shot today.

September 19, 1881. James A. Garfield died at Long Branch today at 10:00 p.m. and buried at Cleveland September 26.

September 26, 1881. Went to Cleveland to attend President Garfield's funeral. Left station at 5 a.m. and returned at 5 p.m.

December 16, 1881. Discontinued the light at this station this morning. Cedar Point not lit tonight and Huron, Green Island have not been lit for several nights on account of the snowy weather. No boats except the American Eagle *have passed this station for 8 days. The lake is covered with ice and the ice on the bay is 7 and 8 inches thick.*

December 27, 1881. No vessel having been sighted during the past week, the light at this station was discontinued this morning.

December 29, 1881. At 6:30 tonight I heard the sound of a whistle on the lake. Therefore the light at this station was relit at that time.

March 25, 1882. Steamer Golden Eagle *sunk by the ice in 24 feet.*

May 18, 1882. Steamer American Eagle *exploded her boiler about 2-½ miles N of this station while racing with the steamer* Jay Cooke. *Four of the crew were killed and all of the passengers were badly scalded (two died—total 6).*

July 26, 1883. Drowned, George McGee, Jr., youngest son of George and Hannah [sic] McGee. Aged 17 months.

March 21, 1885. Today 118 teams passed this station with wine, fish, etc. from the islands to Sandusky and return. Teams drawing heavy loads have been crossing from the islands to Sandusky for the past nine weeks. The 118 teams counted today were those passing both ways. The mercury has indicated zero or below on thirty-three different days during this past winter. The ice on the lake is from twenty to thirty inches in thickness, clear and solid. Several times the mercury indicated 16 degrees below zero.

March 23, 1885. About thirty teams passed the station on the ice today for Sandusky from the islands. This will be the last of the crossing as the cracks are opening.

March 26, 1885. This is the first day since last fall warm enough for the bees to fly. Mercury 56 degrees above zero.

This 1896 USLS print illustrates the layout of the lighthouse, the keeper's house and outbuildings. *Courtesy of the National Archives.*

> *April 25, 1885. A large field of ice passed down this p.m. Last of the season.*
>
> *May 9, 1885. Heavy wind, rain, hail and snow squalls all day.*
>
> *September 10, 1885. Heavy dead sea rolling on the beach this morning. NE. There has been no NE wind for several days. Yesterday the wind blew a gale NW. Last night the wind was light westerly and this a.m. SW. Fine misty rain last night and today. The surf rolled up on the grass.*

Inspector's reports continued to note improvements and repairs at the lighthouse:

1886. Marblehead, Lake Erie, Ohio.—A veranda was built in front of the kitchen, the walk leading from the dwelling to the barn and boat-house was rebuilt, the boat-house was moved 150 feet to the southward, and enlarged, and new boat ways were built and bolted to the rock face. The board fence enclosing the site and right of way was replaced by a wire fence with iron posts placed on the line of the recent survey, and minor repairs were made.

The McGees continued to keep track of lake traffic and their service:

January 28, 1887. Eagle *broke her wheel in the ice near Kelley's Island.*

January 29, 1887. Exhibited the light at this station for the Eagle *last night. She was delayed in coming out of the bay yesterday p.m. and did not arrive at Marblehead until dark. She layed to an anchor until daylight this morning about ½ mile SE of this station.*

March 7, 1887. Steamer Norwalk *and tug* Annie Robertson *towed the* Eagle *into Sandusky today.*

June 1, 1887. US. Lighthouse tender Haze *passed in Sandusky at 9 a.m., came to off this station at 4 p.m. and cleared at 6 a.m. bound up. Commander Gridley, Captain Baxter and Engineer came ashore. Made inspection and left supplies.*

July 26, 1887. Lighthouse keeper H.A. Lyman of Cedar Point came to this station this a.m.

February 23, 1888. The steamer American Eagle *which has been layed up the past 30 days for repairs to her boiler and machinery came out today, passed this station at 5:00 p.m. up the lake. The light at the station was relit today.*

February 13, 1889. Discontinued the light this a.m. as the Eagle *will not be out again for a few days.*

March 2, 1889. Relit the light again tonight after having been out 17 nights. The American Eagle *has been hard off this station this p.m. and working her way through the ice from Put-in-Bay to Sandusky. She could not be seen from this station on acct. of fog.*

March 3, 1889. The American Eagle *was again seen this a.m. off Cedar Point shoreline. Has been laid up in the ice all night.*

August 15, 1889. The stmr. B.F. Ferris *which has run on the Sandusky, Marblehead and Catawba Island route the past 20 years left for New Baltimore last night to which place she has been sold.*

August 17, 1889. The new side wheeler stmr. A. Wherle Jr. *came out on her first trip today.*

August 20, 1891. 18 years ago today I took charge of this station.

In 1891, the Village of Marblehead was incorporated, and the Danbury Peninsula began often to be referred to as the Marblehead Peninsula. An inspector's report noted a new oil storage unit constructed at the lighthouse:

1891. Marblehead, on northeast end of Marblehead, Lake Erie, Ohio.— The metalwork for a circular oil house, which was procured by contract, was taken by the tender from Cleveland, Ohio, and delivered at the station, together with the cement for the foundation and brick lining. The metalwork was put together at the station and placed upon a concrete foundation, prepared upon a rock surface, and it was lined with brick. The oil house was located in the rear of the tower and between it and the dwelling.

In 1892, George McGee's health began to fail. It declined until he died on June 30, 1896, at the keeper's house. Johanna McGee succeeded her husband after his death. She was the second woman to take the helm at the Marblehead Lighthouse. Johanna McGee oversaw the operation of the lighthouse for the next seven years and, during those years, accomplished many things. Johanna McGee and her capable daughters wrote many of the entries after 1894. Included in those entries are a lengthy trip George McGee took through the southern United States in an effort to improve his health:

May 1, 1894. The keeper has been confined to the dwelling by sickness since March 23rd and today he was able to be out of doors a short time. During the past month the keeper has had a man employed to do painting, clean the lamps-lens and at his own expense. His daughter Mattie has had entire charge of the lighthouse.

October 11, 1894. George H. McGee, Keeper of this station, left this morning at 10 a.m. on Str. R.B. Hayes for the South on account of ill health.

December 28, 1894. Large floe of ice came from up the lake today. Small schooner passed this station at 4:15 p.m. and became fast in the ice near Cedar Point.

December 29, 1894. Str. American Eagle towed the same schooner, Maple Leaf, from Cedar Point, passed this point at 3:30 and up the lake.

June 2, 1895. The Keeper returned to this station 2:00 p.m. after an absence of 8 months less 7 days in the Southern states for the benefit of his health. The following route was taken. To Sandusky–Cincinnati– St. Louis–Mississippi River–New Orleans–Gulf of Mexico–Tampa– Deland–Titusville–Cape Canaveral–Enterprise–St. Johns River–

The Marblehead Lighthouse, October 1897. *Courtesy of the USCG.*

The lighthouse in 1885. *Courtesy of the National Archives.*

Jacksonville–Savannah–Atlantic Ocean–Baltimore–Washington–Pittsburgh–Cleveland–Sandusky–then to Marblehead Light Station, his health has been benefited by the trip, although he passed through a very severe winter in Florida.

September 16, 1895. During the past week the tower has been whitewashed, it required 4 bu. lime, 25# salt, almost 5 bbl whitewash, one man in boatswains chair 31-¾ hours of the balance of the time was consumed in mixing whitewash and waiting on the man aloft.

June 30, 1896. The Keeper George McGee died at this station June 17, 1896, age 45 years.

July 8, 1896. Mrs. JoHanna [sic] McGee has this day been appointed keeper of this station.

November 3, 1896. Wm. McKinley was elected president. Marblehead went 19 Rep. majority something never known before.

In 1896, carpenters erected a woodshed and began work on the barn near the keeper's house. As commerce on the Great Lakes continued to increase, Sandusky became a hub of maritime activity. Ships were constantly being towed to yards in the city for repair and rebuilding after meeting with the nasty temperament of the lake, especially in the area of the islands, where many reefs posed danger to ships and their crews. Both steamers and sailing vessels regularly floundered and sank in the waters of the South Passage, often in sight of the lighthouse.

For more than a century, the nation's lighthouse keepers wore no standard uniform. Each keeper at each station wore what worked best for him or her, personally. In 1884, lighthouse officials began an effort to create a uniformed, professional appearance among its employees. "It is believed that uniforming [sic] the personnel of the service, some 1,600 in number, will aid in maintaining its discipline, increase its efficiency, raise its tone, and add to the esprit de corps." On May 1, 1884, the following regulation went into effect:

The uniform for male keepers and assistant keepers of light stations…will consist of coat, vest and trousers and a cap or helmet. The coat will be double-breasted sack with five large buttons on each side—the top ones placed close to the collar the bottom ones six inches from the bottom hem, the others equal distance between them. The length of the coat to be the extended arm and hand; the coat to be provided with two inside breast pockets and two outside hip pockets; the latter to have flap so arranged to be worn inside the pockets if desired. Each sleeve to have two small buttons on the cuff seam, ½ inch apart, the lower button one inch from the bottom of cuff.

The above is only about one-sixth of the directive, which laid out, in excruciating detail, exactly how the uniforms were to be constructed, including fabrics, stitching, insignia, buttons, etc. In 1885, the Lighthouse

Board reported to Congress that it had paid for the initial uniforms for all 1,600 keepers at the 673 lighthouses that currently operated in the United States. After that, keepers were required to pay for their own uniforms. The Lighthouse Board provided circulars, indicating where uniforms could be purchased and the associated costs.

A full uniform, if it were made in Philadelphia, cost $26.25. In today's dollars, that would be about $640. At the time, it equaled about three weeks' pay for the average light keeper. Regulations laid out strict rules for ensuring that keepers always wore the proscribed uniform while on duty. The threat of not wearing the proper uniform while on duty was clear—dismissal. The one notable exception that exempted a light keeper from wearing the uniform was if she was a woman. While it is true that many women had tended the nation's lights, including the second keeper at Marblehead and the soon-to-be keeper Johanna McGee, none was required to wear a uniform.

This vintage postcard depicts the lighthouse prior to the installation of its new lantern at the turn of the century. *Courtesy of the Ottawa County Historical Museum.*

Chapter 6
A TALLER, MORE MODERN LIGHT

Beginning in 1897, the Marblehead Lighthouse entered a phase of significant change, the most obvious being the construction of a watch room. Later, a new lens and lantern were installed. In August, stone for new tower windows arrived, along with red brick to frame its picturesque double hung windows. During the years of change, Johanna McGee faithfully tended the light:

> *July 13, 1897. Three water spouts were seen on the lake today.*
>
> *July 17, 1897. Two more have been sighted, a meteorological phenomenon, is the first witnessed here.*
>
> *September 27, 1897. U.S. Lt. Tender* Haze *passed down this 3:00 p.m. Re'cd from the Engineer's office Lighthouse Depot, Tompkinsville State Island, N.Y. three lamps measurements include height from base to focus 15-³/₁₆ in. diameter of ring 7-³/₄ and the old lamps are to be returned. Inspected Oct. 4, 1897.*
>
> *November 4, 1898. Mr. Fred Barker and Ed Gamble arrived here this a.m. from Put-in-Bay to put up a water hoist on the top of the tower for hoisting up water, to put up carriage house, new stairs into cellar and other minor repairs.*
>
> *December 6, 1899. Seven cases of small pox at Lakeside. All public places have been ordered closed by the Board of Health.*
>
> *September 4, 1900. Lampist finished work on lens today and the keeper left for Adrian, Mich. with her daughter Hannah to enter the Academy. Left the station in charge of daughter, Alice. SW and very warm.*

December 3, 1900. SW heavy dew. Took off deck and tore out ceiling of watch room.

December 20, 1900. The work on the tower was finished today until further notice, and the fixed white light of the fourth order is established and light again is exhibited. Sent reports.

August 15, 1901. Returned from Galion today on the Str. Eagle, *Str.* Washington *came off this station this 12:30. Major Symons inspected station, ordered the keeper to have a Terra Cotta cap put on the kitchen chimney, also to have the dwelling painted as soon as possible.*

September 7, 1901. NE fresh breeze. President McKinley shot at Buffalo, Friday 4:30 P.M. September 6, 1901 by Leon Czolgsz, not fatally wounded.

September 10, 1901. SE gale. President's condition much improved, and is believed will recover.

April 26, 1902. NW gale. A fearful storm is raging. The Schr. Barklow from Marine City foundered half mile from Put-in-Bay. Capt. Pardy, wife and son drowned. The body of Mrs. Pardy washed ashore at Put-in-Bay. Dick Bunk, a sailor, survived and taken to Sandusky on tug John Monk.

The 1897 work on the tower was an engineering feat. A September 6, 1897 *Sandusky Daily Register* article described the work as very difficult: "The iron lantern on the tower, which weighs about ten tons, is now suspended in the air seventy feet above the ground while the top of the tower is being removed to give room for a new brick top which forms a watch room with shelves, closets and circular stairs to the lantern." The addition created space below the lantern where the keeper could perform many of the tasks required to keep the lighthouse in operation, as well as spaces to store many needed supplies and tools.

Before the watch room was constructed, the project included the building of a second tower within a tower. This second, cylindrical brick tower would be used to support both the new lantern that soon came to Marblehead, and the new, larger lens it would receive several years later. The brick tower, unlike the original limestone structure, did not taper as it rose but maintained its circumference from top to bottom. The new brick watch room, which is the last landing that visitors stand in before walking out onto the gallery deck, is actually the top eight feet of the new cylindrical brick tower. During the 1898 work, four window bays were cut into the original tower, and each was fitted with double-hung windows. The windows are situated from the

These iron stairs replaced the original wooden steps, which were constructed of pine. *Author's photo.*

ground up, providing various views as one ascends the spiral staircase. This period of change also saw the construction of a new spiral staircase made of iron. Previously, the lighthouse still maintained its original pine staircase, as called for in the 1821 construction contract. After lowering the existing lantern onto its new foundation, the lighthouse retained its same height, as noted below in an inspector's report from 1898:

> *1898. Marblehead, west of entrance to Sandusky Bay, Lake Erie, Ohio.—The old stone masonry of the upper 8 feet of the tower was replaced with a vertical brick wall inclosing a watch room, furnished with closets and a cleaning shelf. Iron stairs from the watch room to the lantern, four windows in the tower and two in the watch room were provided. Repairs were made.*

While the Marblehead Lighthouse underwent renovations, the nearby lifesaving station continued to serve mariners on the lake. By the turn of the century, the Point Marblehead Life-Saving Station often posted a man at the lighthouse to keep an extra watch on vessels coming and going. Such was the case on November 27, 1900, when a member of the nearby lifesaving station crew witnessed the *Charles Spademan* and the *Melvina* being towed into Sandusky by a steam barge. With winds topping thirty-five miles per hour and waves cresting higher than fifteen feet, the two schooners being towed met trouble at the Cedar Point jetty. The beach patrolman made for the lifesaving station on his bicycle, sounding the alarm and launching onto the lake with six sailors. Captain E.L. Griesser later described the four-mile trip to the Cedar Point channel as the roughest and most perilous he ever made in his twenty-four years of service.

The crew of the *Melvina* were rescued first as they clung to rigging. The lifeboat became grounded on a sandbar a good distance from shore, so the crew helped sailors wade to shore. In one instance, a lifesaving crew member carried a female cook to shore. The crew members then turned their attention to the *Spademen*, where the captain, his wife and four sailors awaited rescue. During that rescue, the lifeboat lost its rudder, and it was eventually towed to Sandusky by the tug *John E. Monk*. The vessels carried 601,000 board feet of lumber and 500,000 feet of lath, much of which was lost. The *Sandusky Daily Star* reported:

> *The life-saving crew which did such gallant work is comprised of Capt. Griesser, Jeremiah Tracy, William Harmony, Jacob Knoerle, Isaac Sauvey, Theodore Pokey, and John Novotny.*

Last night they were wet, tired and cold, after an exceedingly hard day's work. They had little to say, but vesselmen gave them unstinted praise.

The members of the crew spent the night at the Lake House and this morning were towed in their life boat to Marblehead.

While the 1898 work did not bring significant aesthetic change to the Marblehead Lighthouse, the installation of the new lantern certainly did. After the close of the 1900 shipping season, additional brickwork was added to the tower. The United States Hydrographic Office released a notice to mariners that on November 20, 1900, the fourth order fixed white light at Marblehead Lighthouse would be discontinued, and a fixed white lens lantern would be exhibited in its place until planned improvements were completed. These improvements included the installation of a new—or, at least, new to the Marblehead Lighthouse—lantern and parapet atop the tower. The lantern had originally been installed at the Presque Isle Light Station, which was popularly known as the Erie Land Lighthouse or the Land Light. The Erie, Pennsylvania site, two hundred miles northeast of Marblehead, hosted three lighthouses, one of which is still standing but not in use. The original light was constructed in 1812. After the first two towers suffered structural failures in their earlier years, the last tower was constructed in 1867. It was the original home of the lantern that now tops the Marblehead light. The light at Erie was discontinued in 1880 and sold, but, in 1885, it was purchased by the government and reactivated. It operated until December 26, 1899, when the light was extinguished for the final time. The lantern was taken to the Buffalo depot, where it was stored before being sent to Ohio. It was shipped to Marblehead in 1901. While Marblehead received the lantern from the Pennsylvania lighthouse, it did not receive the lens. The existing Marblehead lamp and fourth-order lens were reinstalled after the lantern work was completed. It wasn't until the arrival of the lighthouse's second Fresnel lens—a much larger, third-and-a-half-order lens—that the Marblehead Lighthouse's actual light would change. A 1901 inspector's report noted the new lantern:

1901 Marblehead, west of entrance to Sandusky Bay, Lake Erie, Ohio.—The fourth-order lantern was replaced with the third-order lantern taken from the discontinued main light-tower at Erie, Pa., to increase the power of the light. Some 43 loads of cinders were placed in the driveway leading to the public highway for its improvement. Minor repairs were made.

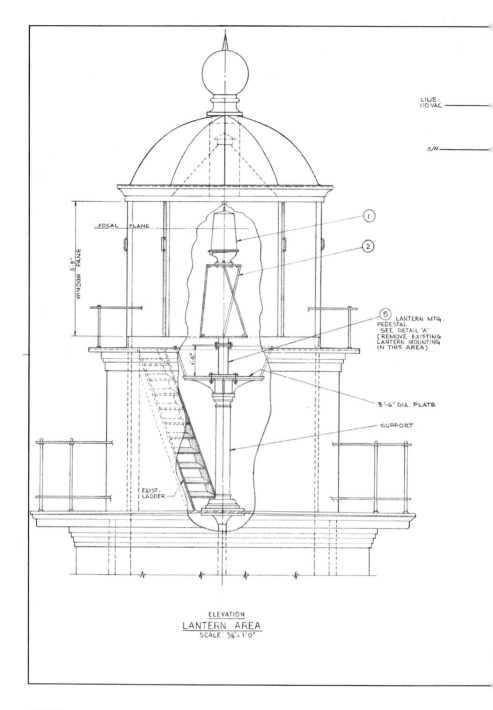

ELEVATION
LANTERN AREA
SCALE: ¾"= 1'0"

A USCG architectural drawing of the current lantern. *Courtesy of the National Archives.*

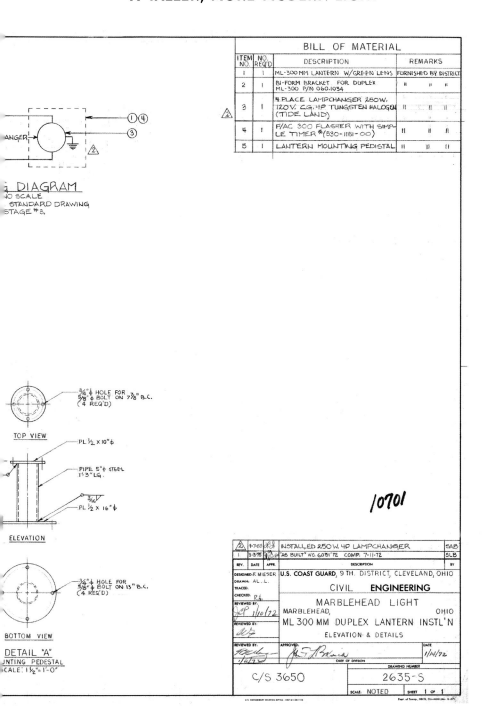

BILL OF MATERIAL

ITEM NO.	NO. REQ'D	DESCRIPTION	REMARKS		
1	1	ML-300 MM LANTERN W/GREEN LENS	FURNISHED BY DISTRICT		
2	1	BI-FORM BRACKET FOR DUPLEX ML-300 P/N 060.1034	"	"	"
3	1	4 PLACE LAMPCHANGER 250W, 120V. C.G. 4P TUNGSTEN HALOGEN (TIDE LAND)	"	"	"
4	1	F/AC 300 FLASHER WITH SIMPLE TIMER #(530-1161-00)	"	"	"
5	1	LANTERN MOUNTING PEDESTAL	"	"	"

DIAGRAM
NO SCALE
STANDARD DRAWING
STAGE #3,

ANGER

3/4"∅ HOLE FOR 5/8"∅ BOLT ON 7 7/8" B.C. (4 REQ'D)

TOP VIEW

PL 1/2 X 10"∅

PIPE 5"∅ STEEL 1'-3" LG.

3/16

PL 1/2 X 16"∅

ELEVATION

3/4"∅ HOLE FOR 5/8"∅ BOLT ON 13" B.C. (4 REQ'D)

BOTTOM VIEW

DETAIL "A"
MOUNTING PEDESTAL
SCALE: 1 1/2"= 1'-0"

/0701

2	4-7-88		INSTALLED 250 W. 4P LAMPCHANGER		SAB
1	3-3-75		"AS BUILT" WO. 6031'72 COMP. 7-11-72		SLB
REV.	DATE	APPR.	DESCRIPTION		BY

DESIGNED: F. MIESER
DRAWN: AL. L.
TRACED:
CHECKED: R.N.
REVIEWED BY: 1/10/72
REVIEWED BY:
REVIEWED BY: 1/6/72
APPROVED: CHIEF OF DIVISION   DATE 1/14/72

U.S. COAST GUARD, 9TH. DISTRICT, CLEVELAND, OHIO

CIVIL   **ENGINEERING**

MARBLEHEAD LIGHT
MARBLEHEAD,   OHIO

ML 300 MM DUPLEX LANTERN INSTL'N

ELEVATION & DETAILS

C/S 3650

DRAWING NUMBER
2635-S

SCALE: NOTED   SHEET 1 OF 1

This Rick Henkel map shows the visibility range of the Marblehead Lighthouse's new lens in 1903. *Courtesy of Rick Henkel.*

The new Fresnel lens dwarfed its predecessor. Manufactured by the Paris company Barbier, Benard & Turrene, the lens weighed a hefty 1,200-plus pounds and measured about 48.0 inches in diameter with a radius of 14.7 inches at the center bull's-eye. In 1903, the new bivalve lens, which resembled a large clamshell, was installed. The lens featured two halves, each with fourteen-inch-wide concentric rings of virtually flawless glass. When the light rotated over the village of Marblehead, the whole town was lit up.

The new light featured something else new to the lighthouse: a clockwork mechanism. Research into the origins of the pedestal, which displays a manufacturer's plate that reads "L. Sutter & Cie.," indicates it was manufactured prior to 1871. It likely came from the Erie lighthouse and was retrofitted for use at Marblehead. What became of the lens that had been in the Erie Land Lighthouse is not known, but it was not installed at Marblehead like the lantern and the pedestal were.

The new clockwork mechanism offered mariners a white flash that lasted for half a second every ten seconds. Previously, the light had shone constantly. To accomplish the ten-second flash, the lens was set on the pedestal and powered by a forty-pound weight. The weight's pull operated a set of brass gears that turned the giant lens around the single-flame lamp. Each time the smooth bull's-eye crossed the flame, the half-second flash was produced. The weight ran the length of the tower and dropped through a fifty-four-foot cast-iron tube affixed to the outer edge of the staircase. To keep the light flashing, the weight had to be hand-cranked to the top of the tower at least once every four hours. The new lantern featured a copper roof. Inside the lantern was a sheet-metal, cone-shaped cowl over the lens, a precaution against any possible leaks in the roof of the tower. Subsequent improvements at the Marblehead site were noted in inspectors' reports:

> *1905 Marblehead, west of entrance to Sandusky Bay, Lake Erie, Ohio.—The metal work for a square iron oil house was purchased.*
>
> *1906 Marblehead, west of entrance to Sandusky Bay, Lake Erie, Ohio.—An iron oil house, with a capacity of 540 gallons, was built. A concrete walk was laid from the oil house to the walk leading from the keeper's dwelling to the light tower. Various repairs were made.*

In 1910, Congress abolished the Lighthouse Board and created the Bureau of Lighthouses, which had complete control over the United States Lighthouse Service. In 1912, the new Bureau of Lighthouses instituted a policy "to promote efficiency and friendly rivalry among lighthouse keeper, a system of efficiency stars and pennants has been established."

The bureau offered keepers inspector's stars if he or she was commended for efficiency for four quarterly inspections. A commissioner's star could be worn if a keeper earned an inspector's star for three years in a row. Efficiency pennants were also awarded to stations that demonstrated the highest efficiency each year. Keeper Edward Herman was awarded an inspector's star in 1939.

One of the most memorable keepers of the light was Charles A. Hunter, who served for thirty years. There are many accounts of "Cap" Hunter's artistic ventures, which included music composition, needlepoint and storytelling. Hunter was a generous and competent host, tour guide and representative of his beloved Marblehead Lighthouse.

Hunter was one of five brothers, all Great Lakes ships' officers. He began his career as a deckhand aboard a ship his brother Silas captained. His

The lighthouse in June 1911. *Courtesy of the Ottawa County Historical Museum.*

larger-than-life character as light keeper is explained, at least in part, by his prior inclinations. According to his obituary, before tending a light on Lake Erie, Hunter was both a prospector and cowboy in the far West.

Hunter was appointed keeper on March 16, 1903, after Johanna McGee concluded her service. The transition is simply marked in the lighthouse log: "March 16, 1903. Mr. Chas A Hunter, Asst. Keeper of Thirty Mile Point Lt. Station, reported at this station for duty to succeed Mrs. G.H. McGee as keeper."

But the transition for Johanna McGee, who was forty-nine at the time, was not that simple. Apparently, she was "encouraged" to resign. While a newspaper article indicated she was to be supplied with an assistant, it never happened. Instead, her ability to operate the new light, which would have included the clockwork mechanism, was called into question. Almost four decades after the fact, Johanna's granddaughter Anesta Rhodes Ludd transcribed a news article to Edward Herman:

In conversation with a prominent citizen of Marblehead and of the lighthouse inspector of this district said: "There is no lighthouse in my district of which better care is taken than this one. Everything is kept in excellent condition." The new light put in this winter requires a good deal of strength to operate, in fact the strength of a man, and it is thought to be too much for Mrs. McGee to undertake. She leaves not because of any dissatisfaction regarding her services, but because of the arduous work connected with the new light. She will quite likely receive a transfer as soon as an opening can be made. At present her goods will be stored and she will make her home with her daughter, Mrs. Dr. Rhodes, of Port Clinton. Mrs. McGee and family will be missed by a wide circle of friends in the community.

Hunter, like the McGees, kept the log filled with information about the lighthouse, happenings at it and around it and current events in the nation:

January 15, 1904. Senator Mark Hanna died at 6:40 in Washington on the 15th.

November 8, 1904. Election day.

November 20, 1904. Ship Phillip Wick *burned off of Huron. Sighted from here at 1 o'clock on the 20 in the a.m. Crew escaped to Sandusky in a small boat.*

December 31, 1904. Bay bridge burned so that trains are stopped from going across.

January 28, 1905. Received large shipment of light supplies, including a second order burner, glass chamber, ball bearings, driving shafts with clutch, brass funnel with strainer, drip pans and other items.

October 1, 1906. Been 5 years in light-house [sic] service today.

February 28, 1907. We have had cold weather through this month lots of ice in the lake teams came across from Kelleys Island today. Ice is 14 inches thick off the light at this date. Was down to basketball game to Danbury. Good game.

August 4, 1907. Gov. Harris cavalry 60 horses and men arrived at Erie Beach.

February 9, 1908, Drown between 3 and 4 P.M. off Smiths Pt. Mike Weable age 15 years. Pete Studid age 12 years.

March 26, 1908. Launch broke down and drifted by the light at 12:20 on the 26th called the life saving crew, picked them up 4 miles from here half full of water in quite a sea. There was two men in launch, Ed Stuide, and Frank Wick, both fisherman.

July 22, 1908. Keeper absent to Put-in-Bay Regatta.

July 31, 1908. A very bright star, East from the light. Looked like an air-ship, seen to-night [sic].

September 18, 1908. Keeper reports the region is very smoky due to forest fires in Michigan.

October 31, 1908. Keeper reported his winter coal shipment arrived from the government, 14 tons of anthracite coal.

February 14, 1912. Wolves seen halfway to Kelleys Island on the ice this p.m.

February 21, 1912. A terrible blizzard blowing a gale with snow continued blowing large snow drifts.

February 24, 1912. Elpha lost his team through the ice in Sandusky Bay Sunday.

November 6, 1912. Woodrow Wilson and Thomas R. Marshall elected President and Vice President of the U.S.

July 28, 1914. Austria declares war against Serbia. Backed up by Germany.

August, 5, 1914. War started in Austria, Belgium, England, France and Germany.

April 6, 1917. Received salary for the month of March. United States declared war on Germany.

America's entry into the war, some three thousand miles away, had an impact on the Marblehead Lighthouse. On March 31, 1917, Hunter wrote in the log, "Put up 4 signs (No admittance to Light House grounds)."

During Hunter's years at the light, it's evident that he was a tough man to work under. Four assistants came and went. Clinton Egelton served just two months, April–May 1903. Charles Perry served from 1903 to 1906. Earle Mapes served just a few months also, October–December 1906. Andrew Turinsky served March–April 1907, when Mapes returned, remaining for six years. In October 1913, Edward Herman became the assistant light keeper. Unlike the others, he remained. In fact, Herman was the assistant keeper for the rest of Hunter's long career.

Herman came to the lighthouse with experience as a Great Lakes sailor. His brother Charles, just a few years earlier, had sailed the Great Lakes on the tender *Crocus*. Edward Herman sailed the Great Lakes on the *Rosedale* before joining the United States Revenue Cutter Service. By 1907, Edward Herman rose to rank of master-at-arms before leaving to join the United States Lighthouse Service.

While Hunter and Herman kept the lighthouse in tip-top shape, they also spent their hard-earned money helping the United States war effort. On June 8, 1917, Hunter wrote, "Keeper and Asst. purchased each $100 Liberty Loan Bond." During that time, Lighthouse Service bulletins encouraged employees

This undated photo was likely taken during World War I. The sign matches the one keeper Charles Hunter erected in March 1917. *Courtesy of the Ottawa County Historical Museum.*

These submarine chasers at the Matthews Boat Company in nearby Port Clinton in 1917 were destined for war. Hunter mentions watching locally made ships heading up the lake in the November 1917 log entry. *Courtesy of the Ottawa County Historical Museum.*

to support the war with bond purchases. The pair's patriotism came at a steep cost—in 2015 dollars, each bond would cost a little more than $1,800.

And while the war raged on thousands of miles away, the pair saw evidence of the great struggle across the Atlantic Ocean. On November 7, 1917, Hunter wrote in the log: "8 submarine chasers passed by at noon."

Those wooden ships, at about 110 feet in length, were manufactured at the Matthews Boat Company in nearby Port Clinton, about ten miles west of the lighthouse. They were headed for war. The company, located on the Portage River, was contracted to build the ships for the United States and submarine chasers for the French. In addition to the ships, the company constructed hydroplane hulls for the war. The keepers made no mention of seeing any wooden planes flying past the lighthouse.

On January 1, 1917, snow began falling in the area. The lake was frozen when three boys headed for Kelleys Island on foot. While the day began warm, about thirty degrees, conditions soon changed for the worse. The boys became disoriented and then lost. By January 4, the temperature had dropped to four degrees, and a blizzard bore down on the lake. One boy was found alive, but the other two vanished into the blizzard.

On January 18, Assistant Keeper Herman located the two remaining boys, who were frozen to death. Hunter recorded in his log, "Asst. found two boys frozen at Put-in-Bay." The very next day, Herman left for Tonawanda, New York, on an eighteen-day leave of absence. Three days later, Hunter reported in the log that temperatures had dropped to seven below zero and that conditions were the worst ever recorded on the peninsula.

While in New York, Herman said goodbye to his cousin Louis and his brother, Charles. Both were leaving for military service and would soon travel to Europe to fight in the Great War. Herman's cousin would not return. The twenty-one-year-old was killed by a sniper's bullet in the trenches of the European front in mid-August.

The next month, Hunter and Assistant Keeper Herman's wife were appointed solicitors for the Fourth Liberty Loan. Just a few weeks later, Hunter wrote in the log, "Bulgeria [sic] surrenders."

In May 1918, a district inspector sent out a memo to keepers on water supplies. The memo instructed lighthouse employees to be sure to place wire strainers over downspouts leading from roofs to cisterns to keep out debris and also to be certain that roofs remained clean at all times. Fortunately, Hunter and Herman never experienced serious issues with clean water supplies, because a good well had long supplied fresh drinking water. However, they did have trouble with a sewer drain that ran between the limestone crevices into the lake. The drain, they reported to inspectors, occasionally backed up.

In October, Corporal Charles Herman suffered grave injuries from a gas attack. The *North Tonawanda Evening News* reported that Herman had been hospitalized in France for several weeks, blindfolded and unable to speak. He was then transferred to a hospital in England. The war ended a month later, and Charles Herman returned home soon thereafter. Because of the injuries he suffered in the mustard gas attack, he never again sailed the Great Lakes on a lighthouse tender.

Charles Herman came to the lighthouse in the months following his return from the Great War. He was married in New York in May 1919, and he and his new bride came to Marblehead for their honeymoon. Keeper Hunter recorded in the log, "Asst. brother and wife arrive for a visit."

The previous month, Hunter had recorded the following entry: "Asst. planted a walnut tree, a memorial to cousin killed in the war!" There are currently several large black walnut trees at the keeper's house, though it is not known which, if any, is the original tree planted in memory of Louis Herman.

An October 1917 inspection by District Superintendent M. Gardner found everything at Marblehead satisfactory. He wrote, "Station in first class condition."

Over the years, Hunter's log entries featured plenty of interesting items, including a submarine arriving in Sandusky in 1919, a keeper on West Sister Island being gored by a bull, a South Bass Island hotel burning to the ground and a balloon passing overhead. In 1922, Hunter began keeping track of the number of visitors who showed up at the lighthouse. On one August 1922 weekday, he counted 260 visitors. On a subsequent Sunday, 130 automobiles parked at the lighthouse.

Hunter was a man of many interests. In addition to tending the light, he was an able carpenter and frequently constructed models of the lighthouse. He also created intricate ship and boat models from wood and once built a fourteen-foot boat that he and his stepson often used in their angling endeavors.

Hunter kept very busy, as lighthouse keepers must, during the shipping season. In fact, Hunter kept busy for his first seventeen years as keeper despite being a bachelor. A 1920 *Sandusky Register* article titled "Lighthouse Keeper Anchored" details, in grand fashion, Hunter's situation:

> *Mr. Hunter for seventeen years kept a bachelor existence as keeper of the United States lighthouse here. For seventeen long years he has been busy by day at cooking, washing dishes, sweeping, dusting—all alone, and during 6,205 long, dreary nights, he has kept the light burning brightly, warning the lake sailors to avoid the treacherous shoals around the Marblehead Peninsula. He was lonesome, longed for companionship, but being of a…retiring nature, he could not speak his sentiment, but leap-year evidently came to his assistance and now that lonely period is at an end and Hunter is happy.*

Hunter and his wife, Elizabeth, hosted a grandson, Mills Brandes, for some years during the 1920s. Brandes fondly recalled many stories from his years living at the lighthouse on the Marblehead Peninsula, including his early school years, skinny dipping in quarry ponds and being the best-fed kid on the peninsula. In fact, Brandes recounted to one interviewer that his nickname was "Fat" because his grandmother made "a lot of rolls, cakes and cookies and things." According to Brandes, Hunter was a stickler for cleanliness and often encouraged children in the area to wash their hands by paying their admission to the movie theater on Saturday nights.

In *The People of Ottawa County Volume III*, Brandes recalled the best entertainment at the lighthouse:

Mills Brandes spent his early years at the lighthouse, helping his grandfather "Cap" Hunter tend the light. *Courtesy of the Marblehead Lighthouse Historical Society.*

Now in the summer time, you could swim right there at the lighthouse. Oh, that's all we did. Junior was in the water eight hours a day. He lived nearby, right down the shore, and his dad was the doctor and he was the doctor for the whole peninsula. We swam right off the rocks. Some people might think it would be dangerous but when you grow up here, you're careful. You don't slip but once. You don't do it again.

Hunter was well known for entertaining visitors at the lighthouse. He frequently hosted children from the area and enjoyed teaching them a variety of lessons. Hunter was always ready to provide spellbinding tales about the history of the lighthouse and its keepers, as well as local history, for guests.

In the winter months, Hunter was especially fond of crewel embroidery. He completed more than twenty intricately detailed pieces during his years at the lighthouse. In addition to his handiwork with fibers, he also worked with words. Hunter wrote the song "The Light-House by the Bay."

Charles Hunter, smoking a pipe and displaying one of his many needlepoint works. *Courtesy of the Lakeside Heritage Society.*

Oh the light-house [sic] by the bay,
To warn all sailors away
Of the danger of shoals and rocks nearby
And the light, it seems to say
I will guide you safely on your way
I will guide you safely on your way

Shine, Shine, Shine
At night for the sailors all the time
For a friend in need is a friend indeed,
Shine, Shine, Shine

If you have someone that's dear,
Sailing the lakes this year.
Oh the light is his next dearest friend.
Let's pray he's now near the bay,
And that he will be home to-day, to-day.

Sheet music for "The Light-House by the Bay," by Captain Charles Hunter.
Courtesy of the Lakeside Heritage Society.

So let it blow, snow or rain,
It always remains the same,
The dear old light that's tested and tried.
Found at night to be so true,
And help guide your boy home to you, to you.

Captain Charles Hunter and Assistant Keeper Edward Herman take a break and pose with Mills Brandes, circa 1924. *Courtesy of the Ottawa County Historical Museum.*

More than half a century after his years at the lighthouse, Brandes spoke fondly of his grandparents and one particular habit they had:

> *Well, for one thing Grandma read to me a lot. So did Grandpa. They were both great readers. These carry over in your whole life…I can sit down and read a whole day's newspaper every day. Grandpa did that. When you're on watch,*

you weren't standing there looking at the lighthouse, you're just checking things every once in a while. In between that, you'd be in there reading books.

Brandes was also still keenly aware of what it took to keep the light operating:

What you had to do was—the light was run by weights, like an old grandfather clock is, and you had to wind the weights up on a drum. They were on a cable. And that pull provided the power to turn the light around...And they never allowed it to be fully extended. Because they had to check every two hours to see that the light was revolving every ten seconds, because it produced a big beam as it turned. When you were out on the water, as that beam crossed your eyes, it appeared to flash and that was the whole reason for that light being there, to do that every ten seconds; so there was nothing more important than having that light always on and flashing every ten seconds.

While most of the keeper's logs have been lost to time and many of the historical records regarding the lighthouse have disappeared with the decades, it is perhaps amusing to know that misinformation about the lighthouse has been circulating for years. An article of this period in the *Sandusky Register*,

This formal photograph was taken by a Cincinnati photographer. The subjects in the photo have never been identified. *Courtesy of Rebecca Lawrence-Weden.*

titled "Famous Marblehead Beacon 100 Years Old this Marine Season," reported on historical lighthouse research by a woman involved in "social clubs and civic betterment work." It read, in part, "Inquiry on the part of Mrs. Elwell among the older residents of the Marblehead peninsula, however, disclosed the further fact that J.N. Keyes, father of the late Col. C.M. Keyes, long one of Sandusky's first citizens, was the original keeper of the light." The reporter also indicated that the structure stood one hundred feet tall, and its lens and clockwork mechanism weighed seven tons.

Hunter's meticulous care for the lighthouse was evident. Brandes recalled his grandfather using a bosun's chair when he painted the lighthouse. "Grandma and I would keep a watch on him until he got to the dome, where he placed a ladder at the rim and stretched high to do the lightning rod. Then grandmother would move from the window and leave him to the almighty."

In 1921, Hunter and Herman compiled a list of start and end dates for the light for the last half century. The season almost always began in mid- to late March, though occasionally as early as mid-February. In 1890, the season never ended, and the keeper worked year-round. Sometimes the light stayed on until January or February, although it was most often extinguished by mid-December.

Chapter 7
ELECTRICITY ARRIVES

Sometime after 1910, an incandescent oil vapor lamp replaced the previous type of oil-burning lamp. By the turn of the century, many sources of lamp illumination in the United States were being modernized. While most people don't think of it as a lighthouse, the first location to utilize electricity for lamp operation was the Statue of Liberty on the Hudson River in New York Harbor. The site was first lit in 1886.

After that, electricity slowly made its way to the nation's lighthouses. It arrived in Marblehead in 1923. With the upgrade to electricity, the candlepower of the light soared, from about 42,000 with kerosene, to about 330,000 with electricity. The incandescent bulb's light continued to be magnified through the same three-and-a-half-order Fresnel lens that had magnified the kerosene flame.

A notice to mariners from the Lighthouse Service announced the new light:

Lake Erie—Sandusky Bay approach—Marblehead Light Station—Light to be improved—On the opening of navigation in 1923 the luminous power of Marblehead light will be increased to 600,000 candles. The light will show a flash of 0.3 seconds, eclipse 9.7 seconds.

Hunter noted in his log that workers from Harry Howard Electric arrived on March 12 to work on the new light system. A day later, two electric lamps arrived at the lighthouse. The new electric light was first exhibited

This undated photo shows the lighthouse tender *Crocus* loading supplies. *Courtesy of the National Archives.*

at the lighthouse on March 26, 1923. A few days later, on March 31, Hunter wrote in his log, "The change from oil lamp to electric makes light greater in every way."

Despite the great leap in technology, the lighthouse still required a keeper. And during Hunter's tenure, that included an assistant keeper, from 1903 until 1933.

On May 30, 1932, Hunter noted in the log that his wife died, and on June 1, she was buried. By June 2, Hunter was busy mowing the lawn, white washing, cleaning inside the tower and repairing an electric switch. His last entry was on June 28, 1933, and read, "June flies thick."

When Hunter retired on June 30, 1933, Herman was the obvious successor, and he took over as the new keeper immediately. Herman, well schooled in the life and work of the lighthouse, was a diligent and conscientious keeper.

During the 1930s, according to newspaper reports, airplane races were held at the lighthouse for several years. Thomas Hausmann was seven or eight

Loretta Dykes in front of the lighthouse, circa 1930. *Courtesy of Chaz Avery.*

Left: Captain Edward Herman, keeper at the Marblehead Lighthouse, standing on the tower deck. *Courtesy of Rebecca Lawrence-Weden.*

years old when his family visited the lighthouse, which served as the south pylon for the races. A north pylon was located far out on the lake. In a 2002 interview for the *Columbus Dispatch*, Hausmann described the nostalgic scene:

> *I thought I had died and gone to heaven. We would sit at the base of the lighthouse. The noise of the single-engine, open-cockpit planes would increase as they dipped their wings, almost touching the ground—at least it seemed that way—the other reaching into the sky.*
>
> *The pilots waved as they came around the lighthouse, and off they went to the north pylon, scaring and thrilling us at the same time. They'd come around the lighthouse—I'm not talking about over the lighthouse—around the lighthouse, and then they'd zoom out over Lake Erie. I could see them smiling. The strange thing is the different shapes of the planes in the races. Some were skinny, some were fat, some had two wings, and some had single wings.*

The races ended as World War II neared.

On December 2, 1934, Herman noted that the lake was very low, and the *Lakeside III* foundered within sight of the lighthouse.

A biplane flies past the lighthouse. *Courtesy of the Sandusky Public Library.*

In January 1934, Herman noted receipt of a new illuminating apparatus, clock and paint. That summer, he spent a great deal of time collecting and disposing of dead fish along the lighthouse's shoreline. On June 29, 1935, the lighthouse tower officially opened to visitors for the season.

In a *Peninsula News* article from 1977, Herman's tours were fondly recalled:

> *Only a few at a time could go up the next ladder to the great prismatic light. Mr. Herman's curt command, "Don't Touch" was always strictly obeyed and all stood breathless as he described the great dome that shot off a splashing spectrum of color and magnified the light…this great light, on clear nights, could be seen as far away as Lorain, and it flashed red in so many seconds.*

The newspaper reporter also wrote of buying homemade bread from Mrs. Hunter and having once been given a kitten that Mrs. Herman was glad to be rid of.

While Herman kept busy tending the light, the lighthouse and the grounds, he was also busy tending to visitors. According to personal correspondence, in 1938, the lighthouse hosted about twenty thousand visitors. Herman kept track through the use of a visitor's log. Interestingly, decades before a lighthouse museum or lighthouse historical society existed, some had already considered preserving the lighthouse through such means. The granddaughter of George and Johanna McGee was one of them. In an August 1940 letter, Anesta Rhodes Ludd wrote to Herman:

> *Mr. Herman, do you have pictures of the past keepers? Might be interesting to start a little museum to be kept there, your historical data, photos of previous keepers, the old lanterns or lamps, chimneys, linen towels for cleaning the chimneys, pictures of the lighthouse before and after changing the lantern and alterations on the property, etc.*

The United States Department of Agriculture's Weather Bureau kept Herman up-to-date with daily weather forecasts that were mailed to the lighthouse. The September 2, 1937 forecast, received at 11:30 a.m. that day, called for "partly cloudy to-night, Friday cloudy with probably showers; continued warm."

CHANGING HANDS

Herman maintained the lighthouse until 1943 and was the last civilian keeper. He, like Hunter and McGee, spent 30 years at the station. Herman built a home in Lakeside after his retirement. After Herman retired, the USCG took over operation of the lighthouse and provided personnel for the operation and maintenance of the 121-year-old beacon.

A full enclosure was constructed on the observation deck of the tower sometime after Herman left. It was used by members of the Ground Observer Corps, a unit of the U.S. Air Force's civil defense programs. Boy Scouts and members of other youth civic organizations kept the tower manned during the earliest years of the cold war, constantly on the lookout for Soviet airplanes or submarines invading America. It was also used for a short time by USCG personnel to observe the growing number of boaters on the lake. It was removed in 1956. A *Toledo Blade* article on the lighthouse's 134th anniversary that year includes photos, one of which is a shot of the tower. In the photo, the observation deck is completely enclosed and features windows all the way around.

In 1958, the lighthouse beacon was automated with the installation of an electric time clock. Up until then, the light was turned on and off manually each day.

Right: The Marblehead Lighthouse in March 1956. *Courtesy of the National Archives.*

Below: A USCG Auxiliary member directs traffic at the 2014 Lighthouse Festival. *Author's photo.*

In 1969, the lighthouse received an extensive makeover. The USCG contracted the William H. Kelley Co. of Detroit to completely strip and resurface the tower. In a weeks-long project, workers painstakingly chipped away the old cement shell, exposing the original limestone that William Kelly—no relation to the operators of the William H. Kelley Co.—had set 147 years earlier. After a thorough sandblasting, a new coat of cement was applied to the structure, utilizing a method that pressurized the application. A total of eight coats of vinyl paint were applied to the new cement surface after it cured. Any loose stone or bricks around the windows were replaced.

During the project, workers commented on the surprisingly good condition of the lighthouse's original limestone tower, considering the century and a half it had been standing. Over the years, the lighthouse has undergone some minor cosmetic changes but has essentially had its Greek Revival elements preserved.

Later that year, in December, the lighthouse was placed on the National Register of Historic Places at the recommendation of the Ohio Historic Preservation Office. It is now maintained by the National Park Service. The designation protects the site from encroachment or possible destruction from any projects or developments tied to federal funding. While a listing on the register is not foolproof, it does provide a barrier to hasty developments or possible razing of buildings or sites associated with structures that have the designation.

After sixty-five years of service, the Fresnel lens was retired and shipped to a USCG storage facility in the Detroit area. The USCG installed a 306-millimeter beacon with green glass (to distinguish it from air beacons). The flashing light was visible for seven miles.

Lifelong resident Robert Boytim recalled the sad day when the Fresnel lens was removed. But the lens didn't stay in Detroit long. A few years later, a small group of Marblehead residents made the trek to Detroit to retrieve the lens after convincing USCG officials to donate the vintage glass lens system to the village.

In *The People of Ottawa County Volume I*, Robert Boytim described both the removal of the lens and its retrieval:

> *It was 1968, somewhere in there. The Coast Guard said it was too expensive to run the light in the lighthouse, and they were going to tear it down. Everybody got up in arms. We wrote to our congressmen, senators, local people, the mayor in the village. They finally said, well, they'd keep the lighthouse, but they were going to take the lens off of it. The prisms*

This Fresnel lens was the second such lens installed at the lighthouse. It is now on display at the Marblehead Historical Society's museum and gift shop, located in the keeper's house. *Author's photo.*

were about four feet in diameter and about three and one half feet high. It was built in France in the late 1800s and brought over here and put in the lighthouse. Originally, they used kerosene to illuminate it. They went to electricity. They used a one hundred watt bulb to illuminate it. It showed 10 miles. All through Marblehead, you could see that sweep when it came through. It was red originally, then they changed it to green.

I think it was in '69 that they decided to take the light out—1970, somewhere in there. They took it out of the lighthouse up there, and I climbed the tower and tried to coax the guy not to take it out because it was such a landmark. He said he had orders, he had to take it out. They put it on the fifth floor of a warehouse.

The village council and the mayor wanted the light, so we wrote to our congressmen, senators, 6th District Coast Guard and we finally got permission to take it. Frank Merrill, superintendent of the Water Works, Jim Menier, councilman, and myself, President of the Board of Public Affairs of the Water Department. We went with the Water Department truck to pick it up. We took bales of straw, blankets, rugs, anything to protect the prisms. We went up to the fifth floor of that warehouse and brought it down. Packed it all up and brought it back to Marblehead. We set it up in the town hall, put it all back together. It sat there for a few years, then the Coast Guard built their new Coast Guard station. They asked us if we could have it there. The village lent it to them (it's still village property) and they have in on display there now.

In late winter, the thick ice blanketing the limestone surrounding the lighthouse melts away. *Author's photo.*

In 2003, there was interest in moving the five-foot-tall, three-hundred-pound-plus lens again—this time, back to the lighthouse it left more than three decades earlier.

In 2004, it was turned over to the Marblehead Lighthouse Historical Society (MLHS), which promptly made a home for it in the keeper's house. The massive lens is currently on display at the MLHS's museum and gift shop.

As early as the late 1960s, several civic organizations were eyeing the keeper's house as a possible destination for relocation, though nothing came of such plans. The Ottawa County Historical Society received an interim license to operate a museum in the eight-room home in 1970 and originally had plans to renovate the structure.

In about 1972, the Ohio Department of Natural Resources began maintaining the property surrounding the lighthouse. During particularly harsh winter storms in 1972, 1973 and 1974, the massive windows atop the lighthouse were damaged. The lake's continuous pounding from its 250 miles of open water eventually led to chipping and cracking on the nine glass plates. At this time, the panes were nearing a century in age. Each pane was forty-six inches wide and eighty-two inches tall and weighed 135 pounds.

New panes were installed in the bitter-cold January temperatures. The local newspaper ran a feature that included photos of men desperately struggling to hoist the panes, with the aid of ropes and pulleys, to the top.

The early 1970s almost saw the complete destruction of the keeper's house. At one point, local fire departments planned to burn the nearly century-old home for training purposes. Accounts indicate bales of hay had already been set against the foundation in preparation for the next day's training when a reprieve came, and the structure remained. Subsequent years saw the structure in disrepair and the target of occasional vandalism.

Chapter 8

A BEACON OF TOURISM AND ART

In 1985, the USCG opened the tower for tours for the first time in decades. Although the lighthouse was open on just a handful of occasions, the tours were a great success. News accounts indicate that at least two thousand people were turned away due to lack of manpower to conduct tours, which were performed by USCG members stationed in Marblehead. In 1987, a number of large boulders, some as large as five tons, were arranged on the shoreline at the lighthouse to protect against erosion and lake-borne debris.

During the next several years, USCG officials worked with auxiliary members and private organizations to open the lighthouse for regular tours. Sometimes it worked out, sometimes it didn't. By 1995, the issue was still a seesaw matter, with different outcomes year to year. Various factors, including staffing and liability insurance, were involved in the troubles.

WOLCOTT HOUSE

While the first keeper of the Marblehead light had faithfully kept the light until his death, he also kept a home about 2.6 miles southwest, just a few hundred yards from the Sandusky Bay. The home was certainly a handsome structure for early nineteenth-century settlers. It is considered an excellent example of colonial hall and parlor design.

An Ohio historical marker at Benajah Wolcott's home on the Marblehead Peninsula. *Author's photo.*

In 1989, the Ottawa County Historical Society purchased Benajah Wolcott's original stone home from a local family who had lived there for years. The Keeper's House, as it had been known for decades, was not in great shape. In fact, the thirty-nine- by twenty-five-foot stone house had undergone many changes over the years, though no major structural changes had been made to the home. What changes had been made were for the benefit of those who had lived in the home over the years, and not all readily lent themselves to an accurate representation of the past. Windows, porches, fireplaces, chimney, rooms, cisterns and other amendments had been made and unmade over the many decades.

Wolcott's stone house served as the family's home after the lake froze over and the shipping season ended each year. Kelly, the same stone mason who built the lighthouse, constructed the house in 1822. He built the home with limestone quarried on Wolcott's property.

Benajah and Rachael Wolcott's residence as it looks today. The nearly two-hundred-year-old home is host to dozens of reenactments, community events and historical activities every year. The home has undergone extensive restoration. *Author's photo*.

Before being purchased by the Ottawa County Historical Society, Benajah Wolcott's home had been occupied for decades. The home was subsequently turned over to Danbury Township. Each year, thousands visit the site for picnics, tours and historical reenactments. *Author's photo*.

The home, with walls about two feet in thickness, is an early example of Federal architecture on the American frontier. The building features heavy, hand-hewn timbers of chestnut, oak and walnut. The main support beam beneath the home, running lengthwise, is thirteen- by nine-inch by forty-three-foot white oak, more than thirty-eight cubic feet in mass. A ceiling beam of black walnut running the length of the home is twelve by twelve inches by forty-three feet.

Sometime in the past, a restaurant, which operated for many years, was added to the home. After being abandoned for more than a decade, the Louis Keller family purchased the property and lived there until the mid-1980s. When the Ottawa County Historical Society (OCHS) purchased the property, it was overgrown with shrubs, vines and weeds and in general disrepair.

The OCHS hired Cleveland-based Gaede Serne Architects, Inc., (GSA) to perform a thorough analysis of the structure. GSA was thorough in its assessment, especially when it found no evidence of a barn or significant outbuilding dating to the home itself:

> In fact, one wonders how the Wolcotts managed their agricultural endeavors in the years 1809–1812 and 1814–1822 when that was the mainstay of their existence. Might there have been a small barn, of logs or of sawn lumber?

While the 975-square-foot home suffered minor structural issues, those interested in the historical, educational and proper use of the property soon restored it to near-original condition.

Today, the home and associated property serves the community as faithfully as it served Wolcott and his family over the years. Danbury Township owns the home, surrounding property and nearby Battlefield Park, the site of the 1812 skirmish. The Keeper's House and an adjacent outbuilding are integral parts of community events, war reenactments, historical programs, celebrations and educational presentations.

Artist Ben Richmond and his wife, Wendy, lived in Marblehead and operated a gallery for more than three decades, creating and marketing a variety of lighthouse-related and nautical works. Richmond's first lighthouse painting was the one that defined his career.

"I was just spellbound by it," Richmond said. "The loneliness of it, the forlornness of it." That first painting, *The Watchman's Gone*, was one of Richmond's two best-selling prints. Over the years, thousands of prints of the lighthouse, the keeper's houses, ships, boats and other associated subjects

Union officer Brian Porter instructs the men in his Civil War reenactment company at the Wolcott house. The restored home of Benajah Wolcott is owned by Danbury Township and operated by the Ottawa County Historical Society. *Author's photo*.

The lighthouse has been an economic engine for the Marblehead Peninsula for years, and its popularity continues to grow. The annual Lighthouse Festival draws thousands every autumn. *Author's photo*.

135

Above: State Parks naturalist Dianne Rozak addresses an eager crowd preparing to climb the steps and check out the view in October 2014. *Author's photo*.

Left: The Marblehead shoreline is often shrouded in fog. *Author's photo*.

were sold. Many avid collectors eagerly awaited the next release of a Ben Richmond piece.

Richmond agrees with others about the reasons for the lighthouse's popularity. First, it looks like what most people think a lighthouse should look like, and second, unlike most lighthouses, it's easily accessible. The unfettered public access makes it an ideal site for picnicking, photography and relaxing.

In 1992, Richmond volunteered to create the artwork that adorned the license plates of hundreds of thousands of Ohioans over the years and raise millions for Lake Erie research. Richmond completed the artwork for the special plates, which featured the top portion of the Marblehead Lighthouse tower, in less than a week.

On June 17, 1995, the United States Postal Service issued a set of five commemorative stamps for its "Lighthouses of the Great Lakes" series. Each first-class thirty-two-cent stamp featured a lighthouse. The series, created by Toms River, New Jersey artist Howard Koslow, featured Marblehead from Lake Erie, Spectacle Reef from Lake Huron, Thirty Mile Point from Lake Ontario and Split Rock and St. Joseph lighthouses from Lake Superior.

While it has served as a beacon of warning for Lake Erie mariners for almost two centuries, the Marblehead Lighthouse is rarely the site of crashes and groundings. However, the site does occasionally receive unfortunate visitors, such as the captain of this boat in 2010. *Courtesy of Dianne M. Rozak.*

MARBLEHEAD, LAKE ERIE
1995

In 1995, the United States Postal Service issued a series of commemorative lighthouse stamps, including a set of first-class Great Lakes stamps. The Marblehead Lighthouse was featured on one of the stamps. *Author's photo*.

While residents and area leaders lobbied for a first-day issue ceremony at the lighthouse, they were disappointed by the USPS's decision to hold a ceremony elsewhere. But for what it's worth, fans of the four other lighthouses were equally disappointed. The USPS chose to hold the ceremony aboard the USCG *Mackinaw* in Cheboygan, Michigan. Second-day issue ceremonies were held at each of the five lighthouses. The event in Marblehead was well attended, with more than two hundred showing up to participate.

In 1995, USCG Auxiliary members operated lighthouse tours, which included trips to the top. That year, 8,181 people climbed the steps to the observation deck.

In 1996, the USCG declared the lighthouse "excess property," a move that freed the agency of the ownership burden. Federal law gives first priority to other federal entities, then state and then local governments and, in some cases, even private organizations. Many lighthouses in the nation have been purchased by or donated to private historical and preservation organizations.

In April 1998, Ohio governor George Voinovich announced the state's acquisition of the lighthouse and the creation of the state's seventy-third park. Both the village of Marblehead, which had hoped to turn the site into a municipal park, and the Ohio Department of Natural Resources (ODNR), had sought ownership of the lighthouse. The ODNR already owned and maintained a portion of the surrounding property, which included the Keeper's Home, a picnic area and a parking lot. The USCG affirmed its commitment to operate the lighthouse's navigational beacon as a necessary aid to Lake Erie navigation. During a period of several years, the USCG also

Above: The USCG's current Marblehead station is located near the site of the nation's first official lifesaving station, about a mile west of the lighthouse. *Author's photo*.

Right: Enthusiastic visitors await entry to the lighthouse during the 2014 Lighthouse Festival. *Author's photo*.

relinquished ownership of more than a dozen other Great Lakes lighthouses. But wrangling over the lighthouse continued. Village officials decided against ownership and wanted to lease the lighthouse from the state. But the state decided, in the end, not to lease the site to the Village of Marblehead in a deal that would have seen the village operate tours and oversee maintenance. A group called the Marblehead Historical Conservancy successfully lobbied against local control of the lighthouse.

That same year, the Marblehead Lighthouse Historical Society, a 501-c-3 nonprofit, was founded to promote the history of Marblehead and its iconic lighthouse.

While there had been discussions and dreams of a museum at the lighthouse since the early 1970s, access to the two-story clapboard house was not realized until 2000. For almost thirty years, the USCG utilized the building as a residence for personnel.

But after moving sailors out in late 1999, the USCG notified the MLHS that it could use the house. Only minor modifications were needed to open up two first-floor rooms to park visitors, now numbering more than one million annually. The earliest MLHS operation included limited exhibitions on Johnson's Island, lighthouse history and Great Lakes shipping history. The MLHS completed its first successful season operating the museum and gift shop in 2000, with more than twenty-seven thousand visitors. By 2002, the museum's popularity had grown, with more than fifty thousand visitors logged.

2002

Dianne M. Rozak has been a naturalist at the lighthouse since 2002. In her position, Rozak oversees the popular lighthouse tours and recruits and organizes volunteers. Each year, she and other volunteers with a soft spot for local history and the lighthouse inform, entertain and guide thousands of visitors to a much-loved view of Lake Erie.

"It's known as the most-photographed site in Ohio," Rozak said. "It's just such a beautiful place and filled with history; people want to be here, to see it, to touch it."

Rozak spends many days each year educating visitors on lighthouse history before sending them up the seventy-seven steps to the observation deck. In 2014, 19,570 people climbed the steps to check out the lighthouse and the view from above. And while those who hike to the top of the tower are counted, visitors to the park itself are not. It is estimated that more than one million people visit the tiny park on the tip of the peninsula. In addition to being a tourism hot spot, the site is also popular among elected officials, both state legislators and congressional members, who make important Lake Erie–related announcements in the shadow of the lighthouse. The Marblehead Lighthouse State Park is open twenty-four hours a day, seven days a week and is rarely without visitors. While the tours to the top and the

The Marblehead Lighthouse State Park remains open to visitors twenty-four hours a day, year-round; the lighthouse itself and the MLHS's museum and gift shop are open to the public during many hours in spring, summer and autumn. *Author's photo.*

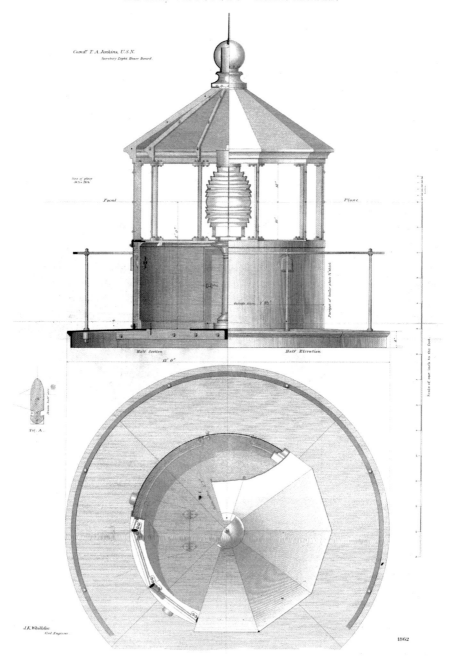

This United States Lighthouse Establishment drawing illustrates a typical lantern for a fourth, fifth or sixth order Fresnel lens. *Courtesy of the National Archives.*

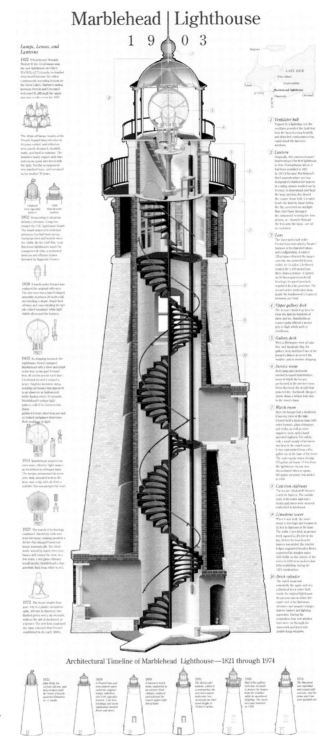

This illustration is the result of years of research by illustrator Rick Henkel. *Courtesy of Rick Henkel.*

Marblehead Historical Society's museum and gift shop have limited hours, the site is open for picnicking, fishing, photography, art and other activities every day.

In 2004, the Fresnel lens that had been on display at the United States Coast Guard station in Marblehead for more than three decades was returned to the lighthouse. It is currently on display at the museum.

In 2007, illustrator Rick Henkel created *Marblehead Lighthouse 1903*. The color illustration, measuring 15 by 34⅝ inches, was the result of more than six years of research. Henkel spent hundreds of hours at the lighthouse, interviewing sources and conducting Internet research and in-person research at various archives.

One of the early insignias for the U.S. Lighthouse Service. *Courtesy of the National Archives.*

"My goal was to make it as clear and understandable as possible," he said. "There were things I tried to nail down factually all the way to the end."

On a single piece of paper, Henkel illustrated the lighthouse through all its major changes, from its original to its present form. He said the most unique feature of the Marblehead Lighthouse is that it was built prior to 1848 and that its original tower is still in use. Most Great Lakes lighthouses built prior to the middle of the nineteenth century have been razed and rebuilt.

In March 2010, the popular band Owl City released a three-minute, fifty-three-second video for its new song "Vanilla Twilight." The video featured a cameo appearance by NBA star Shaquille O'Neal and included a dozen lighthouse clips totaling more than a minute. Several years later, secondary scenes were filmed at the lighthouse for the movie *Wake*, in which Bruce Willis is cast as the main character.

As early as 1983, there were several large cracks in the limestone surrounding the lighthouse. "The Marblehead Lighthouse may someday very well be claimed by the lake water it has protected mariners from since 1881," read a *Port Clinton News Herald* article published in April 1983. The article detailed the concern of the local police chief, who had contacted state officials in Columbus. It is unknown what, if any, actions resulted from the complaint.

On July 1, 2011, a crack discovered in the lighthouse led to the suspension of public tours. The crack was found on the inside of the entrance archway to the tower. Engineers thoroughly examined the structure and found it to be in stable condition. Inspectors determined the cracks developed from natural settling. They neither indicated a flaw nor posed a danger. The lighthouse was closed for only six days and has been open for scheduled tours since.

New Lifesaving Station

Currently, the MLHS is working to establish a new lifesaving station on the lighthouse property. When completed, the twenty-four- by forty-foot building will be an exact replica of the original station commanded by Lucien Clemons, except it will be constructed of modern materials. While the idea was kicked around in the community for years, serious efforts began with fundraising around 1996.

Society members say the fundraising was slow going until about five years ago, when the ODNR began donating 80 percent of the funds collected for lighthouse tours to the group. The entire project is projected to cost about

The USCG's Marblehead Station, July 1947. *Courtesy of the National Archives.*

$300,000. Groundbreaking is tentatively scheduled to begin in 2015. The nonprofit group boasts more than three hundred members from around the nation and currently has about thirty-five active members in Ottawa and surrounding counties.

As the MLHS continues to collect materials, one especially significant item has been secured: the original mortar used at the lifesaving station was recovered from a front yard in the Tampa, Florida area. The mortar had been part of a nautical yard display around a flagpole for years. As it turns out, the current president of the MLHS was approached by a classmate at a school reunion. The classmate, retired from the USCG, had taken the mortar when a commanding officer at the Marblehead station had ordered coastguardsmen to clear out an old storage shed at the then-current station. When the man learned of his old schoolmates' plans to build a replica station, he mentioned the Lyle gun. The initial conversation resulted in the eventual return of the mortar to the Marblehead Peninsula, where its service had begun more than 135 years earlier. The mortar was undoubtedly used many times to rescue distressed sailors.

In addition, other USCG veterans have offered up uniforms, models and other related artifacts. Many citizens have come forward with items to donate. In addition to smaller artifacts, the centerpiece for the new lifesaving station will be a twenty-five-foot, ten-inch motor surfboat. The USCG vessel was donated to the MLHS by a Catawba Island resident who had intended to restore it but found the project overwhelming. The self-bailing boat was in extremely poor condition and had been sitting in an orchard for years. Fortunately, local boat-builder Ned Boytim tackled the restoration project. For the past five winters, the charter captain has been painstakingly restoring the boat by infusing new cypress, oak and cedar where needed. He is working off blueprints from the original construction, obtained from the USCG, and has replaced more than four hundred board feet in the craft, including the steaming of seventy-two white oak ribs into place.

Boytim is using almost all the original hardware in the restoration. Several brass components were cast for the restoration. The vessel contains about 1,200 copper rivets. Another Boytim family member will cosmetically restore the original Buda four-cylinder gas engine. When completed, the

Ned Boytim spent five winters restoring a 1930s-era lifesaving surfboat to original condition. When completed, the boat will be displayed at the new Point Marblehead Life-Saving Station. *Author's photo.*

Thousands of visitors make the trip to the deck of the lighthouse every season. The Marblehead Lighthouse remains one of Ohio's most-visited and loved tourist sites. *Author's photo.*

surfboat will look exactly as it did when it launched from the USCG yard in Maryland sometime in the early 1930s. Prior to its landing on Catawba, it had been used to ferry goods and passengers to nearby Johnson's Island before a causeway was built in the early 1970s.

At the time of printing, the Village of Marblehead, with the assistance of the Western Reserve Land Conservancy, was in the process of attempting to purchase land. That waterfront parcel is about one thousand feet east of the original station, which was located at the site of the current USCG station.

While the lighthouse remains a working navigational aid to mariners, its practical use has diminished in recent years. Satellite positioning, the Internet and other digital products have become commonplace among mariners, from the most inexperienced Lake Erie anglers to seasoned freighter captains.

Just twenty years ago, anglers and recreational boaters most often relied on a compass and the dependable green flash of the lighthouse. But nowadays, mariners rely on GPS units, whether in a cellphone, handheld device or marine electronics. For many in the Western Basin, vision alone dictates trips onto the water, which are nearly always in sight of land.

In 2013, the USCG took yet another step in modernizing the iconic lighthouse. The 150-watt incandescent light that had replaced the kerosene light almost a century earlier was removed. It was replaced with a 20-watt LED, or light emitting diode. The manufacturer of the lighting system, New Zealand–based Vega Industries, paints a bleak future for the usefulness of the world's historic and nostalgic lighthouses. On its Internet homepage, the company clearly lays out the facts of modern technology, "The days of traditional lighthouses are almost over. No longer does a mariner rely on a landfall light

The newest lamp to illuminate the lighthouse is a twenty-watt LED from New Zealand. *Author's photo.*

shining 20 miles out to sea to know his position. Modern satellite navigation systems resolve to within a few metres, anywhere on the earth's surface."

Lighthouse towers are beautiful, but they are costly to maintain. Modern lanterns using electronic sources do not require such structures, require no maintenance and operate more reliably.

The Marblehead Lighthouse remains one of the most-visited sites in Ohio and a favorite of photographers both on land and on the lake. *Author's photo.*

And while the limestone tower holds fast against time and the elements, it has lost its prominence among mariners. As it has shrunk from navigational utility, its thick walls, steady light and classic appearance has proven an invaluable resource to the surrounding communities.

The Marblehead Lighthouse has become an economic engine that is an integral component of the Marblehead Peninsula community, and its importance as a tourism draw cannot be ignored. It is frequently the site of weddings. Some estimates place the number of visitors to the site at more than one million per year.

"It's a draw really from all over the world," said Marblehead mayor Jackie Bird, whose father was mayor when the Fresnel lens returned to Marblehead from Detroit. "It helps the village and our area. I get called quite frequently to perform weddings there, and it's just a beautiful, serene place. We're very blessed to have that beacon in our community."

Bird, elected in 2003, was the first Marblehead mayor to be sworn in at the lighthouse. And, she said, she wouldn't have it any other way.

"I could have done it at a council meeting or in a separate ceremony," she said. "I told them if I had a choice, I'd like to be sworn in there. It was so cold and snowy, but it was just absolutely beautiful."

While Bird was able to quickly convey the intrinsic attraction of the Marblehead Lighthouse's beauty, Rozak framed its popularity with ease. On a recent Thanksgiving, she visited the lighthouse. Rozak met folks from Pakistan and Mexico. "There are lighthouses that are close, but if you're looking for a lighthouse you can actually touch and climb inside, it's a hike. I think the accessibility of this lighthouse has to be the number one attraction."

While the Marblehead Lighthouse is a literal beacon situated on a remarkably beautiful limestone shore, it is also a timeless reminder. The tower remains a testament to the steadfast courage and determination of Lucien Clemons and his brothers and to the pioneer spirit of Benajah Wolcott—a true American patriot and a man with simple vision that he saw and then fulfilled.

MARBLEHEAD LIGHTHOUSE KEEPERS

1822–1832 Benajah Wolcott
1832–1834 Rachel Wolcott
1834–1841 Jeremiah Van Benschoten

1841–1843 Roderick Williston
1843–1849 Charles F. Drake
1849–1853 Lodowick Brown
1853–1859 Jared B. Keyes
1859–1861 W.L. Dayton
1861–1865 Thomas Dyer
1865–1872 Russell Douglas
1872–1873 Thomas J. Keys
1873–1896 George McGee
1896–1903 Johanna McGee
1903–1933 Charles Hunter
1933–1943 Edward Herman
1943–Present United States Coast Guard

BIBLIOGRAPHY

Agard, A.H. "Historical Sketches of Danbury Township." *Fire Lands Pioneer* 10 (1870).

Black Swamp Trader & Firelands Gazette (Port Clinton, OH).

Bowling Green State University, Center for Archival Collections, Historical Collections of the Great Lakes.

Cleveland (OH) Plain Dealer.

Frohman, Charles. *Sandusky Yesterdays.* Columbus: Ohio Historical Society, 1968.

Ida Rupp Public Library. Port Clinton, Ohio.

Keeler, Lucy Elliot. "Old Fort Sandusky and the De Lery Portage." *Ohio State Archaeological and Historical Society Publications* 21 (October 1912): 345–78.

Kugler, Richard C. *The Whale Oil Trade, 1750–1775. Old Dartmouth Historical Sketch Number 79.* New Bedford, MA: Old Dartmouth Historical Society Whaling Museum, 1980.

Lakefront News 72, no. 2 (June 2004).

Lakeside Heritage Society. Lakeside, Ohio.

Lawrence-Weden, Rebecca. "The Lighthouse and the Great War: A Journey Into No Man's Land." *Lighthouse Digest* (September/October 2011.)

Long, Roger. "Keeper of the Light." *Seasons of the Sandusky* (Autumn/Winter 1994).

Mack, Mrs. John T. "Pioneer Days in Sandusky." *Women's Endeavor*, March 21, 1908.

BIBLIOGRAPHY

Matloff, Maurice. *American Military History, Volume 1, 1775–1902*. Boston: Da Capo Press, 1996.

Moon, Paul. "The Keeper, the Builder, the Home." Unpublished essay presented by the Ottawa County Historical Society to visitors at the Keeper's House.

National Archives. Military Pension Files, Record Group 15-A, Washington, D.C.

———. USCG Record Group 26, Washington, D.C.

Neidecker, Betty. *The Marblehead Lighthouse: Lake Erie's Eternal Flame*. Scottsdale, AZ: Inkwell Publishing Services, 1995.

New England Palladium (Boston), February 7, 1809.

O'Connell, Wil, and Pat O'Connell. *Images of America: Ohio Lighthouses*. Charleston, SC: Arcadia Publishing, 2011.

Ottawa County Exponent (Oak Harbor, OH).

Ottawa County Genealogical Society, Archive Collections.

Ottawa County Historical Society, Archive Collections.

Ottawa County Museum, Archival Collection, Port Clinton, Ohio.

Ottawa County—On Page & Stage. *The People of Ottawa County, Volume 1: How We Got Here, What We Did: A Collection of Oral Histories*. Port Clinton, OH: Ida Rupp Public Library, 2002.

Peeke, Hewson, L. *The Centennial History of Erie County, Ohio*. Vol. 1. Cleveland, OH: Penton Press, 1925.

Peeke, Hewson, Lindsley. *A Standard History of Erie County, Ohio: An Authentic Narrative*. Chicago: Lewis Publishing Company, 1916.

Pees, Samuel, T. *Oil History*. 2004. www.petroleumhistory.org.

Port Clinton (OH) News Herald.

Rodabaugh, James H., ed. "From England to Ohio, 1830–1832: The Journal of Thomas K. Wharton." *Ohio Historical Quarterly* 65, no. 1 (January 1956).

Ross, Harry H. *Enchanting Isles of Lake Erie*. N.p., 1949.

Rutherford B. Hayes Presidential Center, Charles E. Frohman Collections, Fremont, Ohio.

Sandusky (OH) Clarion.

Sandusky (OH) Commercial Register.

Sandusky (OH) Daily Register.

Sandusky (OH) Daily Star.

Sandusky (OH) Register.

USCG Auxiliary, Flotilla 16–12, Division 16, 9th USCG District Central Region.

U.S. Congressional Record.

U.S. Lighthouse Historical Society, Historical Archives.

BIBLIOGRAPHY

USS *Constitution* Museum, Research and Collections.

Williams, William W. *History of the Fire Lands, Comprising Huron and Erie Counties Ohio, Illustrations and Biographical Sketches*. Cleveland: Press of Leader Printing Company, 1879.

Wolcott, Merlin D. "Heroism at Marblehead." *Inland Seas* 18, no. 4 (1960): 269.

———. "Marblehead Lifesaving Station." *Inland Seas* 22, no. 4 (1966): 295–300.

———. "Marblehead Lighthouse." *Inland Seas* 10, no. 4 (1954): 274–77.

———. "Marblehead Lighthouse Supplement." *Inland Seas* 37, no. 2 (1981): 84–89.

Wolf, Fred. Personal correspondence (about Charles Hunter), Lakeside Heritage Society, 1973.

INDEX

INDEX

ABOUT THE AUTHOR

James Proffitt has been a writer for more than two decades, most recently working as a reporter for a group of Gannett papers in Ohio. His verse, fiction and photographs have appeared in dozens of literary journals. He currently covers outdoors and conservation news on a freelance basis. He lives in Marblehead.

Visit us at
www.historypress.net
....
This title is also available as an e-book